This edition published 2014

Copyright Matthew Williamson © 2014

All rights reserved. No part of this publication may be reproduced by any means, electronic, mechanical, photocopying, or otherwise without the prior permission of the publishers.

Prologue.

And so here I stand, fully dressed in my bathtub, with my head pressed against the edges of the cracked open window, sucking in as much cool air as my lungs allow. The cool breeze helps. I think. Truth is I still don't know what sets it all off, just a drawing board of deductions and contradictions of everything and anything that may be okay, and what may bring me here. As it stands I have nothing I can do right now but pretend I know what I'm doing and pray for a placebo effect from the air around me, inbetween rounds of strategically layering the bowl of my toilet with sheets of toilet paper to act as a makeshift silencer so as not to wake the friend I had foolishly invited to sleep over in the room just feet away as my stomach lining mistakes itself for Houdini and his water trick, trying to escape.

It's been ten years now since my illness first reared it's head, and I still don't quite know what exactly is wrong with me. Ten years of probing - both interrogatively and invasively - and injections and blood tests, all to conclude with the universal declaration "I dunno." So I guess this is what this book is for in a grand scheme of things; a collection of stories, blogs and anecdotes from myself and the community of IBD sufferers to help offer an insight into the world, and maybe help any reader, or even one of our writers, gain some understanding of their situation no matter how stressful and discomforting, and find a feeling of hope and belonging that we are not alone, not a single one of us.

1.
The End

I was born and raised in Southport, and as a resident Indiana Jones. Although had a relatively strict upbringing at times when it came to supervision and what I could and could not watch, as I'm sure many a kid from the 90s had due to the increasing outcry and denouncement of the influence of films, music and even parks, that did not stop a budding adventurer with a mission in mind. The day I got a perimeter or exploration made available I would make any excuse to traverse it in the most action-orientated sense possible; walk up the bridge to the shops? Why when I could turn through the side roads and pass through trees and abandoned churchyard and find trinkets and rocks valuable to nobody but myself! Why climb down the stairwell when I could vault over it and shimmy along the edge of the neighbour's garage! If there was an adventure to be found, then you could rest assured I would find it. Often with my Tomb Raider t-shirt shielding me from the thorns. When I turned 10 I joined the Sea Cadets and found myself taking this to a whole other level; now I was learning and training towards joining the marine corps. For the first couple of years this meant largely boot camps, kayaking and seamanship, but as I turned 12 the insurance allowed that I learn how to wield a rifle and similar upgrades, aswell as now we were each allowed to select a specific career module to work towards. I chose the Marine Commandos as it would cure my itch for exploration and my newfound love for the military.

Why am I telling you this summary of youth? Because when I turned 14, my mother and were left running out of time on our rented house and she had found an new affordable place to buy which would be our first property she'd actually own. The downside was that this was in Wigan, some 21 lifetimes (or miles if you wish to be pedantic) away from what I considered my home, and my friends and my school. This would be the year things changed..

To my mother's credit we did talk considerably about the effect this would have, and although we were not the most financially comfortable of families, she and my dad would help pay for train fare so that I could continue my final 2 years at high school without too much disruption that would at this point directly impact my grades, and for this time at least continue to have my friends without having to start my life from scratch, as well of course continuing my Cadet training with a regiment I was already familiar with.

Now by this point of my life, I had already got quite far into development, starting puberty a bit early of 10 going on 11, but now was the time all of the people around me were catching up. And this is where the school turned into an earlier form of man we know as the missing link, and friends became enemies and enemies became.. Greater enemies. People were at the stage where they grew a personality, but not yet at the point where they realised they were allowed one, and thus the year split into distinct factions and without going into Mean Girls territory to summarise; there was the chav denomination - a group of kids who decided having hair was uncool and the look of a lobotomy was so in now. By contrast to them was the freaks 'n' geeks which in my school managed to be broadened to define "people who don't like football", and finally theatre and music who in truth never actually enjoyed each other's company just both had to share segregated territory. Being an avid lover of hockey and rugby (though detester of football) but also devoted fan of Timelords and Star Wars, I found myself in cultural limbo. I had friends on either side so had the rare opportunity to pick my path, and am proud to say I chose the camp of the freaks 'n' geeks as they were the more individualised camp who were more accepting of who they were (within reason; they still had their guidelines of what you couldn't like without being 'one of them' of course. This was high school of course). I bring up this cultural tear as me having a choice and voluntarily allocating myself as one of the geeks, made me an insult to the chav sect, and I was made example of. A lot. From then on if any new person joined and wished to prove themselves, they had to start a fight with me. I had already learned my lesson in retaliation, and developed my own technique; fight back all the pain and make every possible witty retort I could muster in response to the use of a fist, the plan being that if I'm still making jokes and seeming to be having fun with the situation, this demoralises the assailant and they want to stop before looking a fool to the crowd they are trying to impress with the attack. And it's always good challenge to try and top your own punch lines.

So my friendships I had worked so hard trying to maintain during my move were now moving on to different playing fields and I had found myself with just a small band of people to hang around, and an even smaller band of people I felt I could trust. And then I found out one of my friends killed himself. For any of those who have yet to experience the death of a loved one in any capacity, I won't go so far as to say there is not a feeling like it, but it's certainly a rare commodity. It feels a little like at first like the muscles in your face are powering down - it doesn't feel like simply losing a smile, but like the notion of joy itself has suddenly gone flaccid, and your stomach feels like that sensation when you dip your toe on the circling drain of an emptying bath; every fluid is leaving your body and you can feel it gushing for freedom, and the faintest but a very real pinch of the gravity of the situation. Within the same month I lost another person equally close to me, and this gave the bullies ample ammunition. Sure enough I soon started to hear rumours geared towards reaching me about my responsibility in these events. At this point I now had nowhere else to turn; my friends by my mind now were either dying, or busy eyeing me up every chance they thought they could chance to see if they could find a chink in my armour.

I have no idea if this played any part in instigating my problems, but by the centre of that summer, I had my first official flare.

They say you never forget your first, and though this is thankfully a story a million miles away from the topic that expression is actually used for, it is certainly very apt here. My step dad had cooked up a healthy sizing of chilli con carne, which even preceeding this point I had always disliked on the grounds of kidney beans having a distinct taste of a felt door stopper. But on this occasion ten minutes of my stomach feeling conflicting appreciation for being full, whilst sulking over what it was that was filling it up, I felt something punch up into my throat and I immediately made what would be the first of many brisk walks to the bathroom. The pain was unreal and yet very, very real. The food was using my stomach lining as a trampoline as it tried to gain enough momentum to escape, each retch punching organs up against my ribs followed almost immediately a compaction lurching through my intestines. This process repeated for what felt like an eternity (and always does) but in reality was only three before I knew enough to leap off the seat and play musical chairs with my mouth and bottom. I won't deny the tears streaking down my face, both from the pain and the confusion, although I had no immediate cause to assume this would become a lifelong battle I felt like my body was making me atone for my sins as this was an ill I had never felt before…

Nicole Rawkins:
Me and My Crohns Disease

09 Monday Jun 2014

So this is my first ever blog about me myself and Crohn's. This is my third time of writing it too, first one was too boring, second one got deleted as my phone died and this is the third. So let's hope it's third time lucky?

So I'm 20 and have Crohn's disease. A life threatening, life long illness. No cure and hundreds of side effects.

Am I sick? As a bloody chip. But I've gotta keep on going don't i? Can't let this bitch take over my life can I? So I'll start from the beginning when and how I got diagnosed.

Looking back now I've had the symptoms of

Crohn's from the age of about 14-15.

Yeah mad how I only got diagnosed 2 years ago isn't it?

It was my own fault though. The pains I was getting came and went every now and again and because they went away for so long at a time, I forgot about it and never thought anything of it.

Anyway I hit 17 and noticed I'd started bleeding from my bum obviously I thought it was just piles at first but because I knew there wasn't anything hanging out my bum I knew that shit was about to get serious. I knew that the amount of blood that was coming out of me every time I went for a poo was just not normal.

Eventually I plucked up the courage to go to the doctors with my partner by my side. I went and seen my usual GP who was already aware of the history of Crohn's in my family. (My mam got diagnosed in about 1996 and my auntie about a year before me) My GP examined my bum and told me that is was really inflamed. He did this while my partner was in the room. I felt totally violated, embarrassed and horrid. This is something no one should ever have to experience but I guess it was probably the best thing that ever happened to me cause if it hadn't, I wouldn't have ever found out that I have Crohn's.

Anyway after chatting with the doctor about symptoms etc. he decided to refer me to a gastroenterologist straight away. No pussyfooting around. It was at that point I knew that without a doubt I had Crohn's. I told my mam everything and I think deep down she knew too but she didn't want to believe that it was. We didn't really mention it again until the appointment to see my consultant came through. I could see how worried my mam had became but I was still being just not bothered. My consultant felt my tummy and asked loads of questions.

I remember that appointment like it was yesterday because it was red hot outside and even hotter in the hospital and I remember as he was examining me I was sweaty and my skin was all clammy and I felt totally and utterly vile but the more I thought about it the more hot and flustered I got so I just wanted to get out of there ASAP. Eventually the appointment was over.

The outcome? Well it had to be the dreaded colonoscopy. I was 18 and getting a camera UP MY BUM! I was mortified! I had to wait for the appointment for that to come through the post but before that I had to go into the hospital for my pre assessment and get all my Bowen prep and stuff oh and so they could sit and talk me through this lush procedure I was going to have. I mean it made me feel so much better about it… Not!

So, I think that was the week before or something and then the following week I had to follow this horrendous diet then take loads of laxatives. At the time I was working in a Chinese and they didn't believe that I needed three days off. Trying to explain this to people that don't really understand English was just impossible! I think I ended up going to work on the same night I had the procedure. Assholes!

Anywayyyy back to the blog, the day finally arrived and I swear when they said my mam couldn't come with me I nearly cried. I felt like I was about to have an operation and felt like a tiny little kid all lonely and ugh it was awful! So I went through trying not to cry I got changed trying not to cry I got stabbed with a needle while they put a cannula in, trying not to cry. Got wheeled into the room trying not to cry and when I saw it was a woman I felt a whole lot better. I can remember lying on my side when she asked my to and my bum falling out the covers and I pulled the blanket over and then realised what's the point so I pulled it back and said 'I might as well leave that out' I mean how bloody embarrassing.

The doctor was like, well we will just cover it up for now. I swear she was trying not to laugh but I was nervous and you say stupid things when your nervous don't you? Anyway they offered me this 'sedation' relaxation drug thing and I thought YES I'LL NOT REMEMBER ANYTHING so I took that thinking yeah buddy and when she told me it was like being stoned I thought minttttttt!

However did it work? NO! I remember everything

I mean every little thing! I was gutted but glad cause I found it totally fascinating. I had to stop writing this late last night and come back to it this morning cause my eyes were burning I was that tired.

So I'll continue. I asked loads of questions as the camera went round and everything looked great until she reached my terminal ileum and there it was a very small piece of inflamed bowel. I asked what that meant and straight away she said, I suspect it's Crohn's disease. I was so glad that I finally had answers and that something could now be done about it. I wasn't scared I was more excited to get started on some meds so my symptoms would bugger off.

After that I had another follow up with my consultant and we decided azathioprine was a good medication to start on. I refused steroids and I still do because I already struggle to lose weight with the Crohn's alone and don't want to end up any fatter because of avoidable meds. Another reason why I refused them is because I know it's only a short term fix.

My mam was on and off them my whole life and

she was great while she was on them but as soon as she came off them she was back to square one. To me that seemed pointless. Anyhow I started the azathioprine and all was going great until three weeks into taking it I had to go to A&E.

It was June or July I think I know this because it was the morning of the air show and I wasn't missing it! I went really early in the morning so it was pretty quiet and I got seen pretty quickly. The doctors were bamboozled as they couldn't figure out where the pain was coming from. It wasn't until they took some bloods that all became clear. The nurse came in and said your bloods have shown pancreatitis. I was like what the hell is that? Haha! She explained that it was inflammation of the pancreas but couldn't understand how I had it as I didn't drink. She came and went about four times. I was demented.

Jonny googled if my meds could have caused it and apparently they could. So we told the nurse when she came back and she was like ohhhhhh yes. Like duh! You should have known that anyway. You're the doctor. Not us.

So as time was getting on I said to her look I need to go but I promise I'll come back if I get any worse cause I wasn't missing the airs how for no one! She discharged me on the condition that I did some back if I got any worse. I was like look, I'm not stupid! I'll come back if I get any worse. So I got my discharge papers and off I toddled.

My nana and jonny were with me that day because my mam was away and some motorbike thing. She always goes to them. I asked my nana to give us a lift to sunderland so we could get on the bus to the airs how from there. Because I came well prepared we had all our stuff with us anyway so we didn't need to. Go back home or anything we could just go straight there.

We got there eventually, me high on tramadol and still in agony but I lasted the day just with minimal fun. Like I didn't go on any rides just literally sat and watched the planes. I couldn't even enjoy any food as every time I ate it killed me.

Anyway I'll cut to the chase cause I'm babbling a bit. Told you I babble.

I ended up going back to the hospital either the same day or the day after I can't quite remember whenever it was though I got admitted. I didn't know how long I was going to be in for. I was gutted. I hated hospitals and just wanted my mam and jonny there all the time. The ward I was on was actually really good and let my mam come early on the morning and stay all day with me. So that wasn't so bad. What was bad was how constipated I was it was horrible! That was when I experienced my first enema. Vile things they are but it helped. I was in hospital for three days and was told to stop taking the aza. My Crohn's subsided for a bit then for a good few months. Three weeks of the meds and pancreatitis was well worth it. I'm gunna do this blog in two parts as there's so much to write. This is the end of part one. I'll write the rest soon.

Thanks for reading xxxx

09 Monday Jun 2014

So I'll begin from where I left off.

I'm writing this trying to fight against my burning eyes and fatigue. So I'll more than likely have to stop and come back to it again.

Anyway once I'd recovered from the pancreatitis and my Crohn's had got a little bit better I had been offered a job in a care home. I obviously took it because life was great and I was feeling great I was working all hours over Christmas and life was good until Crohn's popped up again. I wasn't turning up for work because I was so fatigued and feeling crappy, it obviously didn't look good so I managed to get a sick note off my GP. I took it into work, well actually my mam did as I was poorly then about a week later I had a letter through my door saying I'd been sacked.

I was fuming but it was out of my control and there was nothing I could do. So I was jobless. Back on the good old dole. Job hunting again but kind of enjoying the break at the same time. Enjoying the rest.

As time went on my Crohn's got worse, I got more poorly and was constantly at hospital appointments. I was abandoned by my consultant for a year and a half and after continuously pestering my consultant and telling him that something wasn't right and after him telling me for months that all my symptoms were IBS I eventually asked him if I could have another colonoscopy. Yes, I had to ask to have another camera up my bum because I knew something wasn't right.

Previous to that I fell pregnant but had that snatched away from me. I was fed up and needed something to be done. This time I didn't have any drugs during the colonoscopy apart from buscopan cause I started having spazims and I was totally awake and having a good crack on with the doctors (as you do) and he came to my terminal ileum again and there it was, and it had spread!

I wasn't best pleased to be honest. Why hadn't he listened to me! This could have been prevented! What a dick!

Anyway from that I was given some more meds which I am currently on. I'm on methotrexate one and have been for four weeks. So far so good. Jumping back to just after the colonoscopy, I got offered another job at sevacare which I am currently working as a carer in the community looking after the elderly and disabled. I love it! But I'm finding it so hard at the minute trying to fight my fatigue and work. It's becoming impossible but I refuse to let this get the better of me! I will fight and keep fighting until I can't fight no more.

All I want is a career, a normal life and although it seems impossible right now I will keep trying. Good things come to those who fight and be patient. So whenever your feeling down, don't give up!

Im just going tot jump back to my childhood and my mam as i think this is why I'm who I am today and why I'm as strong as I am now. My mam, my hero, my role model and my best friend!

When I was around threeish, my mam was really ill, like almost on her death bed. I was young and didn't understand what was going on but I did know that my mam was poorly and could quite possibly die. She was hospitalised for a very long time and me and my brother were living with our nana and grandad.

I can't really remember much apart from her yellow pyjamas that she wore in hospital, her little teddy that she had which I now have and having awful dreams about her being in hospital. I can remember standing looking in my nanas mirror and imagining her behind me putting her arm around me and just crying for her all the time.

That was a pretty hard part of my life to talk about because I literally lived in fear of losing my mam. Of my mam dying. It was awful. I can't even begin to imagine how hard it was for my mam. She was given two weeks to live and if it wasn't for my nana and grandad paying for private healthcare my mam wouldn't be here today. Eventually after months in hospital she was released with a permanent ileostomy. We lived with my nana and grandad for a bit until she was strong engh to come home. She was on that liquid diet thing which I forgot the name of and I can remember me and my brother drank the ones that she didn't like. My favourite was the chocolate and the toffee. When my mam came home me and my brother had to do a lot to help her and stuff. She even taught us how to change her bag.

There was a point in my life where apparently I would only go to nursery if I had a bag on like my mam. I obviously have no recollection of this but my mam won't stop mentioning it haha!

All my life I lived in fear of my mam dying right up until the point that I got diagnosed and started to learn about the illness and stuff. I still worry but not as much as I used to. My mam is one of the strongest people I know. She is my rock. This is part two of my life story. I will keep blogging but it will be about the present. I hope you enjoyed reading! Thanks for being interested xxxx

14 Saturday June 2014

I write this as I sit here with a glass of wine in one hand and a jar of fluff in the other.

 I've had a few days that haven't been so bad, well apart from being very fatigued but I slept most of the weekend so I'm feeling ok today.

This post is about me, my illness and my partner. So, I met jonny just over three years ago we've been together ever since. Not long after we had got into a relationship, and he'd pretty much moved in to my parents house I started having the first of my bad symptoms. That was when I had started bleeding.

It was jonny who encouraged me to go to the doctors about it, he has literally been there from the day I was diagnosed right the way through my journey and still is of course. He has came to most hospital visits if he has had the time off work and supports and comforts me through every good and bad time.

To be honest, although he understands and has been absolutely great I still feel like a bit of a burden on him most of the time. Because I have pretty much always been ill this means we haven't been able to go on our first holiday together, go places he wants to go with his friends like the V dubs festival etc etc. even down to like going out for a drink or a meal, most times we can't even do that.

We spend most of our time in the house of at my family's houses or very close friends' house but even then that sometimes proves to be quite difficult. There's been times where I've said to him that he's better off without me and that he could have a better life with someone else but not once has he even contemplated leaving me.

Don't get me wrong, without him I probably wouldn't be where I am today but knowing that I'm stopping him from living his life, restricting him so to speak absolutely breaks my heart but

I'm glad I have him today and I'm glad he doesn't want to leave. He's my rock, my best friend and I couldn't have done any of this without him. We just keep telling ourselves 'when I'm better we will do this, that and the other' even though realistically speaking I won't ever be 'better' but I hope one day I will be in remission and free of the pain and suffering. Then we will be able to do what we want when we want and enjoy our life together.

I know some of you may be thinking, why let it stop you etc? We'll let me tell you, my biggest fear of going abroad is ending up in hospital. At the minute I see my Crohn's as unstable and my main focus is getting better. When I'm better I will go onto bigger and better things. Go places we want to go, do things we want to do and be happy.

I think that's all I can really write about this particular subject but I wanted to share with fellow IBDers in this situation that your not alone and to my friends and family how hard it is and how much of a struggle it is. I don't think my relationship has ever been so strong. And the more we go through the stronger we get. Keep smiling and keep supporting each other. Through the good times and the bad. Thanks for reading guys. Until the next blog, much love! Xxxx

2.

Back Alley Medicals

Three Months Later.

Since that first night things had changed considerably for me. What had started off as a fluke bout of hell had now taken up residence in the house. Rent-free I might add. The freeloading illness had become somewhat clingy and co-dependent too, as this was not even just a guest for evening meal, but now every morsel and scrap I would consume whether it be a pizza, a pack of crisps, or even a single bite from a Mars bar, would require a couple of rounds with the toilets; a particular nuisance when it came to my all-boys high school meaning a man has to plan his impulsive bowel explosions in advance to allow for time to make the surrounding area safe for skin contact. Needless to say the meat on my bones was now resembling the level of meat you would expect on a cheap set of Chinese ribs from a dingy takeaway, and my muscle was significantly more fragile. And so now here I was twiddling my thumbs in a dingy back-alley doctor's office; my eyes straining to be intrigued by the informational flyers stapled to the wall - not by nails, but by the grit and grime that comes with such a place - in a desperate bid to avoid sharing any awkward stares from the accompanying misery manifestations that sat creaking in the chairs opposite.

The questions circle the drain around my head; what is it and why me? What did I do to cause this? And though I know now that it is nothing that I did, that never stopped the guilt or the scenarios of possibility racing through my head. This we shall touch on later. I got called in, and my chair and I shared an audible sigh as I stood and scuttled in to the office of the tall and gangly doctor who looked remarkably like Stephen Merchant with bleached blonde hair flicked up on its well-groomed end. He indicated to the chair and I sat and felt my knees begin to dance as he asked me to explain what brought me here.

Given my age, this was the first visit I had ever taken to a doctor's alone, let alone been the key note speaker. And it most certainly did not help that I was trying to tell this man about how I pooped and vomited in as much detail as any procedural show would lead me to believe could be vital information. After a couple of minutes the man held up his hand to signal a willingness for the verbal diarrhoea to stop and we shared a moment. Not a blissful moment, but one of painfully awkward silence before he looked me up once and slowly trawled out "Okay.. If you could lie down here and we shall have a look." Dutifully I hopped onto the bed and fell down onto my back and felt my insides lurch with fear as the gangly doctor loomed over me; his shadow crawling up my skin before a long bony tendril stretched out towards my stomach and prodded at it before retracting. This procedure repeated itself with increasing force over every millimetre of my stomach, a noticeable increase in the tempo as I started to lurch with discomfort, as if he were trying to play me like a rather disgruntled piano. After he had his fill of curiosity he returned to his seat and his face turned solemn;

"Sit up." he paused as I struggled to a comfortable position; my stomach acids (and residual breakfast) bubbling like a mento in coke. "I've had a good look now and I don't think there is anything wrong with you."

There was an awkward silence as I waited for him to go on, but his eyes seemed to say this was worthy of a complete diagnosis. Eventually I tried to prompt a more indepth expression from him;

"So… What does this mean? Like, what could be making me throw up like this, because I can't say I feel too normal right now."

He seemed to ponder resentfully for a moment, before leaning slightly closer and declaring me as a budding anorexic.

I left the doctor's office expressing my fury at the indignation in the most aggressive nature that an Englishman can show; saying a courteous goodbye without thanking them and politely closing the door with as little noise as possible. I'm sure it hit them pretty hard. Walking down the alleyway from the doctor's back to my mum's house, I remember very vividly how quickly my mind was racing through every key buzzword and imagery it could possibly muster up for me to try and figure it all out..

Was it really nothing?
But if it was nothing, then why was I doing it?
But he's a doctor, surely he'd know if there was something?
But then again, he *did* just stab me with his fingers as a test..
…Stupid, bony fingers…
So what could it be? Allergies? Stress? Every bad eating dare catching up to me?
..A stomach failure?
Oh God..

This was largely caught short by the time I hit the door, and my mum asked how it went, leading to a mini tirade of sarcasm focusing almost exclusively on the incompetence of the doctor and the sleazy locale, with only a passing post-it of how it's making me feel. No need to worry someone about my own worries right? I mean that would just be silly, no need to dwell on something like this until there is something to report.

This was my first complete failure of a diagnosis, and it really fucked me up. I had no real ideas on how I should deal with this information, this being only the second really big visit for the doctor's I had required. And I'm pretty sure spending a summer watching Batman would not be quite as beneficial as it had been years previous for my broken arm. The way I chose to handle it I will forever hold as one of my big regrets in life; I chose to bottle it up and repress my secret shame. Coming so soon after becoming public enemy at the school for trying to dare explain my depression and lust for isolation to a couple of close friends, I lost every blink of trust I placed in humanity and as a result I became increasingly aggressive towards people aswell as known to simply disappear faster than Peter Parker in a crisis. I'd start jokingly bully some of my friends, as if trying to project any attention coming towards myself onto those around me, whilst also wanting to maintain the position as being 'the funny one' in my group of friends, and I am not proud of this even to those who took it in good fun. This translated even to my cadets, where before then I was bright and playful child who was just loving anything given to him to do, whether it be manning the masts, or rifle duty, or even when came to cleaning. Now I had become jaded and cynical and downright irritable about my duties, not helped that many of my friends had moved on which meant not only was I now surrounded by people I didn't know at my low point but also all my training had to reset to accommodate the newer recruits; whilst I was waiting to train for 1st Class Seamanship I now had to sit through 3rd Class over again to wait for others to catch up, all the while taking constant breaks to run to the toilet and return considerably lighter and often eyes notably glassier from the battle.

By this point something else was starting to become semi-regular, something terrifying. Charging into the dingy permanently stained bathroom stalls and having to cram my head inches from week old urine which surprisingly paid no assistance to the stomach punching it's way through my diaphragm, my eyes streaming with tears of the excruciating pain, air finding itself trapped in an organic trash compactor that was my throat, and as I looked down into the toilet bowl to asses the damage and found not vomit or the little carrot-like chunks of stomach lining, but blood distilling in the small puddle of water and saliva. Sweat beat out my pores as I stared down at the swirling trickle of blood slowly swirling and forming a milky way in this grim environment, and fear lurched through my body as this went some way to confirm many paranoia's I had suppressed of my illness. Namely that niggling rare possibility of cancer. I know now it seems silly to think of a fourteen year old boy panicking himself stupid about the possibility of dying of cancer, but at the time I had nothing else to go with, I didn't have much in the way of internet resources, a doctor who was very adamant there wasn't any sickness with me despite my constant nausea, surrounded by smokers through a large majority of my life, and now coughing and retching fits that resulted in blood. And still I refused to tell people. Even my mum only occasionally heard of the blood when fear took a firmer hold of me, but always in a passive glazing over to laugh away any sense of threat or fear for her, and for myself.

Now as the years have passed by, I can't be sure on exactly how long since this first incident, but my guess was maybe a month or so after the first blood incident - and several more beside it - I made a decision to leave the cadets and drop my ambition for joining the Royal Marine Commandos at least for now until a cause could be found and then, I told myself, I would get back into training. So now evenings spent previously studying seamanship or kayaking were left with myself, my brain, and my bowel movements. A bitterness began to slowly swell within me as I resented myself for damning myself with whatever I had clearly done to my insides, and I spiralled into a period of depression. I take no pride in admitting to the nights spent just curled in the centre of a double bed crushing my legs into my stomach, streaming with tears and the several nights of contemplating suicide. By the age of fifteen I had taken this contemplation to a more physical interpretation on two occasions; the second of which was the most excruciating which was an overdose on Paracetamol. Obviously it didn't have quite the intended effect - something I am very grateful for almost every day since - and what I got instead was a night of agony.

This is one of the nights I can recall very vividly even to this day on almost every one of my senses, though I am not so sure I am grateful for this. The effect didn't come on immediately and in all honesty a good visual aid for this would be the transformation sequence from *An American Werewolf In London*, as I sat on my bed with *Red Dwarf* DVD set looping in the background as I tried to dull my mind with some light reading, then it hit me. All at once, every nerve in my torso shredded apart like a guitar string being played by a razorblade and I fell from my bed onto the rough and fading purple carpet screaming through every note the blade chose to play. I fought with every muscle in my body to move to my feet so as not to inhale thinning carpet fibres and saliva that pooled from my mouth, but the pain intensified with every twitch of my muscles, so that I simply compromised to getting to my knees and punching my fists into my stomach, as if trying to go mano y mano with the pain. The veins in my temples strained to burst and my stomach started hitting the ejector seat, trying to battering ram its way out of there, and though I had done this out of depression, now I felt truly miserable.

Katelyn Hajnik:

My journey dealing with Crohns Disease

18Jun2014

So one thing I've noticed as I become more active in the IBD community, is that awareness seems to be significantly higher in the UK than Canada and the States. I'm part of a Facebook group called #GetYourBellyOut. It's a fantastic place for everyone with IBD to vent, ask questions free of judgement, and just be themselves…

This morning the #GetYourBellyOut page absolutely blew up with anger and frustration... The BBC news this morning did a whole segment on IBD and how the number of people being hospitalized is increasing quite a bit... You can read the story here.

It starts off talking about how between 2003 and 2013 there was a dramatic increase in the amount of people hospitalized and treated for Crohns Disease. Personally, I'm really not surprised. I don't actually think the number of people developing IBD is increasing. I think people are just becoming more aware that it exists, and diagnostics have improved significantly in the last 10 years. People are also becoming more comfortable in coming forward about bowel issues.

There are tons of people out there who don't want to go to their doctor because they're ashamed, or embarrassed to admit they have a problem. Especially when it comes to a topic like bowel movements, where i swear 90% of the population is to chicken talk about openly.

So here is the rage inducing part of the article… It goes on to talk about the potential causes… genetics, environmental factors, immune system issue, smoking, infection…. that's all well and good… Then this doctor comes along from St. Georges's Hospital in shout-west London…… and says this:

"We know that there are many genes that predispose someone to get Crohn's disease.

"But we also know that lifestyle factors like eating a lot of junk food or taking many courses of antibiotics may make it more likely to happen."

And that's when the UK blew up in a storm of angry…..

I wasn't impressed either when I finally read the article.

First of all, if antibiotics are increasing the number of people being diagnosed with IBD why are doctors prescribing them so much??? I'm having trouble understanding how antibiotics could possible CAUSE IBD…. of course they don't explain their reasoning behind their theory….

But then to say that junk food may also be a cause…. THAT makes me angry….

First of all, there have been times in my life where i survived on junk food… not because I had poor eating habits or anything like that… but because it was the only stuff I could get into my system, and it gave me the energy boost I needed to live what little life I had…

Even 8 months ago.... When all I could manage to get into my system in a 24 hour period was a handful of crackers... it was chocolate bars and candy that kept me going... probably kept me from completely starving to death. My body also seems to have an easier time processing some junk food than healthy food. A Big Mac from McDonalds sits better in my stomach than a handful of broccoli....

If I look back on my own childhood these theories make absolutely no sense... before the age of 5 I had ear infections and asthma, but other than that I was a perfectly healthy kid. I rode my bike all the time with some friends up the street, ran around the yard with my brothers and their friends.... I was fairly active....

Then I think about other people with IBD... there are BABIES and young children being diagnosed.... so how can you say its because of junk food and antibiotics?? Are you suggesting parents are now blending up a Whopper Burger, fries and a shake, lacing it with antibiotics and using it to bottle feed children??

To me, this doctor is basically coming out and saying "you did this to yourself". As IBD patients, we were not active enough, we didn't eat properly, and we took the drugs our doctors prescribed to us… so we brought this on ourselves….

Makes me want to punch her in the face….

I don't believe that there was ANYTHING I could have done differently to change my fate of having Crohns. I'm also not going to sit here and blame my parents and say if they had raised me differently, I wouldn't be struggling with this horrible disease. My parents worked very hard to raise their 4 children and I think they did a pretty f-bombing amazing job!! Even if something they did or didn't do was even a minor contributing factor, I still wouldn't blame them…

Honestly, I don't feel the need to play the blame

game… Yes, it would be fantastic to find a cause for IBD… and finding a cause would do AMAZING things towards finding a cure…. Don't get me wrong, I'm glad scientists and doctors are doing research and spending all this time and money to find a cause and cure… but what does a cause matter to me??

The fact is… I have IBD… I have to live with it, and I'm dealing with it the best I can both physically and emotionally. Personally, I think I'm doing quite well… But finding a cause isn't going to make a difference to me…. What, you found out why it happened so now I can point fingers, and be bitter and angry at someone or something for doing this to me? Why would I want that?

There are some days I use every ounce of my being to stay positive, and have a good outlook on life. I don't want to point fingers and say "you did this to me!"

Maybe that's just my personality coming through…. I tend to not care WHY things happened… just realize that they did, and find a way to move on and persevere. Theres really no point in dwelling on the past… Just keep your head up, and keep moving forward!!

So, now that my rant is over…. Update time!!!

I am currently HATING prednisone…. I am now getting the acne that comes with it… my forehead is breaking out horribly :(I still haven't slept through the night… except that one night… when I only slept for 3 hours… I'm still eating everything in sight…. to the point where I swear my scale has stopped displaying numbers and just says "your fat"…

I realize I'm not actually fat… But I also realize

that I currently (and for the last 8 months) have a very messed up body image… When I weighted about 150lbs i thought and felt like I looked great.. yes, I had my fat days but who doesn't.. I was happy with the way I looked… Then I dropped down to 112lbs. I thought I was a skeleton…. I hated the way I looked… Even now, when I'm folding my laundry, I hold up my pants and think "I can't possibly fit into those…."

Now…. now I'm up to 127lbs and I feel like a freaking elephant…. I think that its mostly just because of how much I've been eating… my stomach feels tight most of the time, and with the prednisone I'm retaining a ton of water and am constantly bloated… But I know that when I look in a mirror Im looking through a funhouse mirror. What my brain sees is not what everyone else sees.

This saturday I resume my taper off prednisone. I'll be down to 6 tables (30 mg) a day… hopefully when I get my test results I can continue my taper.

3.
The Great White Depression

Misery is a funny thing. It can corrupt you to your very fibre, instigate some of the most violent and depraved actions in our human history, bringing out some of the very worst sides to even the greatest of people, but it can also be our saviour. And, as I lay ingesting tacky floor designs, it gave me clarity. To date this suicide fad is the sole time I have engaged in the fabled out of body experience, and I could do nothing but watch as this pathetic and deteriorating skin flake of a body was burying into the floor.
Was this really what I had become?
Was this what I was going to go out looking like?
No. No I couldn't let it end like this.
Cliché as it can sound I'm sure and perhaps even a little hokey, this gave me strength I could feel now ripping up through my veins and I was going to fight against the very solution I had

created for my pain.

I crammed two of my bony digits down to the back of my throat and fumbled around for a gag reflex like a particularly awkward evening at a school disco, and in a similar climax to such experience the lack of technique resulted in a bitterness and bile - though far more literal in this instance than with the analogy - and I started to throw up every meal I had even dreamt of consuming for the past week in a fairly systematic regime. There would be exactly three very brutal impersonations from my stomach of Ivan Drago trapped in a bag, followed by one final sucker punch with a cuisine of choice remained as an odorous babyfood, several tears, and five solid minutes of listening to Chris Barrie and company tease each other over their fond memories on the troubles of *Red Dwarf* before the clock card was punched and the impersonations started again. This carried on long after every last snack and food dream had passed my lips the undesirable route, and from midnight onwards I was puking a thick black tar that I recall deciding was a physical metaphor for all the evil I had suppressed and spewn back at people who only largely deserved it. My mother was working on a night shift at a hospital at this time, so I knew I could reach out if I wanted within a reasonable time frame of her work break period, but I couldn't tell her. The truth is I was scared how she would react. By this time I was long past the point of being a mamma's boy as I was in my youth - we had grown very different sensibilities and she was far more influence by the media outcries of impressionable youth, and I revolted against the idea as if making a personal little *Citizen* Smith of myself buying games and films that took my interest and actively not going out and re-enacting them because of the functioning brain cells I possessed; and if there was a particular controversy surrounding an item such as *Child's Play 3* you bet your ass I was going to be watching that on TV to see if I could justifiably gauge the level of bullshit deflected onto the mediums. That was thankfully about as far as my revolutions went, but just because I had anger towards some of her convictions and held opinions, it didn't mean I ever wanted to hurt her or give her reason to hate and I was very aware at this point that to her suicide was going the coward's way out.

I eventually found my wording and texted her a summary of my pain, something along the lines of condemning the illness and the pain and bile surrounding me, and asked for advice. She messaged back about some remedies we had downstairs in the kitchen, and I thanked her and set about making my plans for the trip to the kitchen. I played it out like a video game; waited for my counter to reset with the next bout of tar, and then set off at full crippled pelt - which is actually as those who have experienced such a recurring vomit session can vouch, is infact 1/3rd of the speed of walking and yet feels like lightning - down the creaking and eternally-partially decorated stairway, and into the kitchen whereby I slammed open the necessary cupboard and half climbed in to raid as much of it as I could. Not to overdose of course, by the very nature of Plan B that would be redundant, but to be able to make sure this time I take everything as instructed and that I won't hinder my recovery any further. I remember taking two boxes with me, but only one has stuck in my mind because even now as I sit at my breakfast bar glancing out at the sunny day staring in on me as I type this, I can't express why this helped. One was a box of some pharmaceuticals most likely to try and constipate me as a hazarding guess, and the other was a bright red packet of strawberry flavoured Strepsils. My logic for taking them was simply so I had something to continuously suck on to get my throat used to the idea of consuming something rather than ejecting it, to prepare for the next phase of sending in the Hovis bravo team for mop up duty, as well as wash the bitter taste of self-contempt from my mouth.

Returning to my room I gauged I had enough time to try and interfere with the time schedule, and so grabbed an open of Fanta and swilled down one pill before slipping in the Strepsil and slowly masticated as the clock wound down for the next trip to the bucket I had propped against my leg like a faithful puppy to his master. Of course as would be expected, the vomit came back as clockwork, and all my tears parachuted into the bucket almost on cue, as if they had braced for impact this entire time, and the Strepsil and I parted ways. But this time as I stretched back and rested my head against the comforting embrace of my mattress, I felt a smile flicker in the corners of my mouth as I wiped the drool from myself; this time I was beating it and I was going to truly take it down now. I was a new man. Just a new, very sick man.

I counted down eternally between every breath of the Craig Charles anecdotes, and when the five minute mark passed by and there was no surge of violence beating within, just a vague irritable swirling - the intestinal equivelant of "Did I leave the oven on?" - my pride got reinforced and when just two minutes later the vomiting returned my smile remained throughout every last bitter heave. I'd count down the retches the same way I always do to this day; like a thunderstorm.

Retch.
One-one thousand..
Two-one thousand..
Hurl.
Retch.
One-one thousand..
Two-one thousand..

Three-one-

Hurl.

Good. The storm is passing. Each time swapping out the extruding fluids for a quick rinse and a fresh Strepsil. Three episodes passed, and finally by the time I had switched to the next series, I managed to make it a full 28 minute episode without even a stir in my belly and though I knew the storm was still visibly raging on, I was now merely observing from over the hills rather than sat directly under the heavy rain, and so chanced a quick few bites of a bare slice of bread for some cleanup work, swabbed my teeth with my toothbrush, and made sure to trick myself into sleep without the concerns of disturbing the stomach acids; sat propped up against the wall down the side of my bed, head lulling to the side and light bright and glaring.

This worked surprisingly well, and over the years has become a practising standard when having particularly bad flare-ups - propped up usually on my couch now that I have moved on to independent living, picking anything particularly placid (noticing anything overtly sexual or violent seems to provoke more gut surges than I would prefer. Not too sure on this one, but my guess would be that it has something to do with how both of those things make your blood flow rush, but don't go quoting me on this fact) and just positioning myself on my couch not quite lying down, but quite sat up and letting my fatigue and gravity tuck me in.

Of course, surviving the night did not make me any stronger the next morning. But I had to maintain that nothing was wrong so as not to perturb my family and risk either lectures against how stupid I already felt I had been, or the alternative of being possibly fairly heavily monitored from what I already disputed as relatively strict upbringing. So, as a result I opted the easiest of the options presented; the 15 minute walk to the train that wouldn't show up, followed by the next 20 minutes to a successful train, 30 minute journey to spend another 10 on an entirely different train, and finally 15 minute walk to school. All whilst feeling frail enough to deserve a drip of some form. I can only imagine the horrors my crypt-keeper form must have appeared to my group as I shuffled into the canteen, but my condition was pretty apparent, evidenced when my friends Ian and Carl diverted me to a shaded corner of the canteen between a holy grail of abandoned steel cabinets;

"Are you okay?" Carl's face looked worried; the raising of his eyebrows adding several decades worth of wrinkling to his features and the contorted grimace of his lips parted his perpetually unshaven look his puberty had gifted him with.

I forced a smile and went to play it off okay, but I couldn't do that, not to my closest friend at the time. So I found a new way to express my feelings; I told him a brief summary of what happened in a somewhat bleak tone and with a mocking sensibility - I was a pawn to be ridiculed for this I saw, and that was made I made of myself. It worked and became something of a running joke in regards to failings - the man who failed so hard at life he failed even to end it. Once again, as with the bullying that started previously, humour became my outlet, and now my own misery was to be my gladiator; scuffed and scraped and thrown into the arena for the amusement of those surrounding me.

I surrounded myself from then on in the company of the group, no more alone time and no more wallowing. People didn't need to know my illness but that didn't mean they couldn't know me. From now on I was diving headfirst into whatever the group wanted to, good or bad, which of course led to the inevitable when considering this would occur not too long after the appearance of shows in the vain of *Jackass* and the like. But whether it was living on the dares of others, or telling anecdotal jokes of my own I was getting laughs and I was loving it - finally I was getting attention again but not for my mistakes, now I was being sought after for being a personality. The next stage of this was to talk with Carl, we had long since buried our original hatchet of fighting to be 'the funny one' of the group and acted as more of a duo, heavily inspired by our own comic legends Adrian Edmonson for me, and the late Rik Mayall for him. As a result we started writing together, creating our own short sketches and slapstick routines we would then perform in front of our friends at the park after school. Shortly on our audience did increase reasonably so that now it extended to not just our group but people who had maybe before now said a running total of two words to us in our entire run of the school, all gathering to watch Carl and I pretend to violently assault each other in increasingly elaborate ways as convincingly as possible. To save this turning too much into an autobiography I won't go into too much detail, but our plans and events were increasingly successful, and we were gaining acceptance from those who had detested us - or at least a placid indifference, but that was certainly an up. Around the same time I found myself gaining notoriety with a small comic strip I was spreading through the school depicting our high school teachers as a variety of inept heroes and villains called '*The Chromosoner*' and a less popular but far more satirical '*HoboCop*' which set to protest my particular stance of the time on extremist political correctness with a character fighting a barrage of stereotypes in order to create a PC World. The latter did get me into a decent amount of trouble to a point where its run was somewhat shortlived, but *Chromosoner* brought my newfound observational and dark humour to even teachers themselves who would begin to request cameos just to be mocked.

Now, as my years at high school were coming to a close, my illness was still burning on and slowly corroding away all remaining fat and physique but my will was pumping enough iron to topple Arnold Schwarzenegger should it wish. I was beginning to feel stronger than I had ever been, even with a past consisting of boot camps and rugby.

Chris Waller
A Brief Bio

Ok, so here's my story.

I'd always been someone who would have "bad guts". I'd get ill when we went on holiday and stress would always lead to problems. I have a vague recollection of never really feeling comfortably "clean" in that respect, if that makes any sense.

Through university, I had a pretty good time but I'd have really bad incidents of vomiting or diarrhoea that I'd always put down to just not being able to hold my drink (I was a student, remember). Ironically, I smoked quite a lot of cannabis at the time and this seemed to mean that I could eat and drink pretty much anything most of the time.

I graduated and went off to work. I shared a house and always had a few raised eyebrows due to my odd diet. I never seemed all that hungry or interested in food and seemed to subsist on whatever high energy stuff I could cram in. My housemates never really realised that my gut problems were getting progressively worse - leading to some truly embarrassing moments that they don't even know about to this day (such as pooing into a bag due to the communal toilet being blocked - nice, eh?).

I managed to get to the point where I could get my own place and no-one quite knew the freedoms that this gave me. But I found that my health was starting to deteriorate. My flaky guts were getting worse and my energy levels were decreasing. I pushed for a consultation (more than once) and faeces and blood tested showed that something wasn't right. Finally, after a sigmoidoscopy I was diagnosed with crohn's in 1999/2000. Ironically, I was relieved as at least that diagnosis meant I wouldn't be getting an ileostomy (which seemed to be the natural course of things) - at least in my ill-informed mind.

I was put on all sorted of drugs - all the usual suspects you'll be familiar with. A routine ultrasound to try and get to the bottom of some localised pain showed up the need for some gut surgery which turned into a right-hemicolectomy in 2001. That went well except for excruciating hiccups for two weeks caused by a bubble near my diagram.

That gave some relief, but I was still deteriorating and living in a kind of limbo - with no energy and no enthusiasm for life. In the winter if 2002 I found that I was feeling very unwell and also developing a lot of pain in my backside. I dodged Christmas and New Year by doing the teenager trick of telling my family I was with friends and my friends I was with family. I returned to work that January feeling horrendous and booked myself in to see my GP (ironically, just as I managed to negotiate a pay rise - not sure how I did that).

When my GP took a look at my backside he diagnosed a large abscess. He gave me antibiotics and signed me off sick. I took the antibiotics and they just brought on horrendous diarrhea. I phoned the doctor and some friends and went off to a&e.

They whipped me through pretty quickly and I had my abscess removed. The recovery from that included the first time I had ever fainted from pain. I got discharged and friends took me home to my own house, but with a bed made up on the living room floor. It was obvious within a couple of days that I couldn't cope and - at the age of 28 - I was collected by my parents to go and stay with them.

There then followed weeks of recovery where I didn't really improve. Something wasn't right. My wound was healing but I was feeling worse and eating even less. I was checked in again to the hospital where another abscess was identified.

I had this removed, but it left me incontinent (abscess was basically growing through my rectal sphyncter). On top of this I was still feverish and unwell.

Weeks in the hospital culminated in me requesting an ileostomy, which I had just days after my 29th birthday in 2003 (just as we invaded Iraq - I watched a lot of that war unfold).

I went through the usual psychological struggles to come to terms with the surgery but my physical recovery was phenomenal. Suddenly I was well - even though in some respects I could be considered disabled.

I returned to work and - at leaf by my standards - threw myself into life. Through work (long, or at least detailed/consulted story) I met someone I fell in love with. I'll gloss over the story but our relationship went from phone/email to physical simply but with some trepidation (if anyone feels it would help, I'll happily elaborate). I proposed to her around Christmas 2003 and she moved in with my in May 2004.

I met my wife through work. We were rolling out a huge piece of software and I went down to london to train the person who was going to be running it at a particular site. Must have trained her really well as we started flirting a lot over email and phone. It got to that inevitable point where we needed to meet up or it would have gone no-where. But before we got to that point I decided that she needed "to know".

Luckily when I say "site" I mean "Guy's and St Thomas's". Luckier still I'd had a chat with one of her colleagues about my condition and recent surgery (he was a senior nurse). So basically, I bottled it a bit and asked her to ask him about it. Not only did she ask him, but she followed it up by visiting a ward and even got to meet a patient who had a stoma.

So she was prepared.

The meeting up went well (wink, wink). She travelled up from London to Chester and stayed for the weekend. We took things slowly and carefully. Everything felt very natural and just worked.

I think things went well because we'd kind of fallen in love already. Also, we never set any expectations. We didn't pressure ourselves to have a physical relationship and just let things happen.

We even had a weekend of her helping me through my first blockage. By 2005 we were married and in June 2006 our twin boys were born.
Now I am pretty much symptom free. I take lanzaprazole for reflux and had a completion proctectomy in 2011.

I wouldn't say I'm physically or psychologically "bang-on". I'm finally building my core up again and I've had bouts of depression and anxiety. But on the whole, I'm good. I have a normal, happy, active life. I have scars, both mentally and physically but the truth is - everyone does. Everyone has stories of battles fought and battles they are still fighting. In some ways I am lucky that mine are easy to poi put out and identify.

I was a bit of a sickly kid, but never really had many doctor's visits for gut problems. I suffered from bronchitis and migraines as a kid and seemed to be on antibiotics a fair bit (I'm allergic to penicillin which added a complication). In uni I didn't really see the doctor much at all. I think as I was trying to get diagnosed the general thought was ibs. It was only when they found blood in my stool and an elevated esr that people thought it was something more. I think quite few family and friends thought I had an eating disorder. There was a tv show on channel 4 at the time about odd eating habits and I started thinking that maybe it was all psychological for me. Then they showed a lad with crohn's who was on tpn and I thought that my symptoms sounded a lot more similar to his than the other people on there.

4.
Sex & Intimacy

So by now I had been dealing with my illness for a little over 2 years, and although had now lost any appeal in sport, my future career ambitions, a collection of muscle, fat and hair, and even my own faith - things were starting to feel up. And I had of course, as had many of this age group, become (somewhat sporadically) sexually active. And again as with many participants in our baser human natures, there are of course a lifetime of anecdotes and sob stories of my own experiences, however a large majority of them are not connected to my illness so I shall spare you of those ones. Some of them however, are.

The timeline on this one is a little more askew so as to not present myself as a slut, and for their own sake of dignity (not over the stories mind, just their involvement with yours truly) the involved females shall be kept in complete anonymity, but I do feel this is an important aspect to express in regards to the illness as it is still such an integral player in our modern media and social hierarchies, but one that to date I have seen no-one address is the problems that could occur whilst trying to tackle the beast of intimacy. And the final disclaimer is that this is of course solely from the male perspective on this one. Right now that's out of the way, let's get to embarrassing myself for education and entertainment..

The first point worth expressing is never, ever have sex during a flare up. You may have the blood pumping through you trying to peer pressure you against this this, and in your time you may meet some extraordinary beautiful women (or men) who would also prefer you ignored this, but don't do it. There are a couple of ways in which this could go very wrong at some incredible speeds, including the simple of only lasting a few minutes in terms of stamina - I am not sure as the science of this but I am unfortunately familiar to the reality and embarrassment of having a holiday with one of my first loves and though my internal organs were Barry White, my stamina had skipped Cds and decided to be more Vanilla Ice. However embarrassing premature ejaculation could be to any man, this would simply be a mild inconvenience you could work around with extended foreplay and positional techniques so it would at least be satisfactory for when you can truly make it up to them when back to regular stamina. No, there are far worse experiences to concern yourself with when it comes to the lifelong question; do I have sex or do I go to the toilet?

It had been a hot summer morning and myself and a girl I had recently started courting were spending our afternoon just strolling through the local town, before the audible sizzling of our skin was beginning to drown out our conversations and we agreed it would be best to go back to the shade of my house and continue our conversation as well as maybe watch a film. Thinking ahead I knew were I to have a guest I was not likely to have any regulation to my meals of the day, as always feels incessantly rude to abandon a guest and get yourself a snack - even if it is demanded of you from your bowels. At this point I had become aware regular eating was a necessity, but was blissfully ignorant that there was very little you could do to work around it by say eating more at one time and waiting longer. No, the stomach has it's own very set timetable on what you will eat and how much and when it is to be allowed. So we took a detour through the welcoming breeze of the local Tesco store and I bought a pack of babybels and a couple of snack bars for myself thinking this would be enough to provide some nourishment but most importantly were all the kind of food that can trick your belly into feeling more full than it actually is, thus staving on any awkward disappearances.

The march home was filled with general back-and-forth (in fairness, this was largely on the forth-front as I recall, my eagerness to impress was definitely allowing something of an ironic bout of verbal diarrhoea) and laughter inbetween gorging my face on my pack of babybels and one of the snack bars doing my pass it off as just a man who enjoys the luxury of eating itself, which was half true - even now, having spent an unreasonable period of the last decade staring down at my food as it remerges from within looking as if it has gone through a faulty teleported and landed inside out, I have never stopped lusting food in all it's varieties and textures. We arrived back and headed straight up the permanently half-decorated hallways to the safety of my bedroom - by this time I was still living with my mother, who was thankfully away at work.

The immediate advantage of my bedroom at this time was that it worked as an excellent gauge on how interested a person was in me, as the door would slowly peel open their eyes would be met with the fraying edges to a very thinly painted sky blue wallpaper; the original underlying salmon pink glowing through with a strong sense of defiance and rebellion not found elsewhere in this teenage boy's room. A feeble attempt to combat this shade of femininity was the torn pages of *Kerrang!* Magazine photos; Marilyn Manson, Red Hot Chili Peppers, Amy Lee and James Hetfield all contorted in various poses around the walls, with the more diverse of interest's hidden away to the sides of bookshelves. The main detracting factor however was not the gender-defying wallpaper, but in the carpet - a thick and very definitive purple welcoming every footstep to tread on it's fluffy surface with a welcoming embrace. Though I stood in the doorway waiting for an excuse to be made, she didn't bat an eyelid as she stepped inside and made straight for the large wooden-framed bed and allowed her body to drape across it - not suggestively mind, no this was the look of someone who felt true comfort.

We spent the first hour of our time watching tv together in that tantalising middle-ground proximity - close enough to be a sign of intimacy but also distant enough to simply be a comfortable friend, and I have never been one to push my luck. By this time I had felt only a small flurry in my stomach but it had been quickly excused by a brief bathroom visit, and I felt confident I had escaped lightly.

I returned to the bedroom with a new confidence filling the void in my intestines, and we talked about her past profession as a dancer, and the underlying curiosities that ran with it, before we moved on to the subject of masseuse. I quite merrily offered these services - I knew this was a skill I excelled at, and was happy to show off a little for a change rather than second-guess every compliment, and so lay her down on my bed, lifting her black dressy top and slowly started to massage in a small collection of oils. Here I got my first rumble of trouble. Just a small yelp of a stomach drowning in it's own acids, and I knew this would signal a wave of nausea to flood my body, but I was not going to pass up this opportunity so chose to ride it out and carry on, and the massaging led to kissing, which led to a very different massaging, and of course led to sex.

Despite her reputation as a dancer, this girl was not the most active of participants in our naked tango, meaning a very definite increase in manoeuvring on my part to try and lead. This was fine for the first 10-15 minutes or so, but soon enough I felt that familiar force emerging inside. I was embarrassingly British about the situation, and rather than tell her the truth - that I am an idiot who neglected his own medical condition to spend the time with her - I faked an early climax, allotted a minute of apologising sincerely through it, before making my excuses and dashing to the toilet 'to clean myself up', apparently for half an hour. The truth of course being having to play musical chairs with the toilet to try and vomit and shit out all of my mistakes for the day, through the silencer of padded toilet paper to mask my shame. Though a silly story to talk about, this was one of the hard hitting cold facts in my life I had to face; there was no tricking this, no talking my way around it, no shortcuts and no distracting. This illness was my body's full blown temper tantrum and I was locked in with it and would have to play by his rules.

Part of what hit the hardest though for me, was the knowing defeat in her face after I returned and we drew a stalemate position of cuddling up on the bed. This was a position she had no doubt been down many times before with guys, and I had wanted to be different and show her a better experience, but sometimes even the knight in shining armour can cause damage on his conquest.

She wound up staying the night, and

propositioned we gave it another go, but frankly I was terrified of a sequel of my own (wouldn't you be if the threat of sex could lead to extended toilet visitation rights?) and so settled on a painfully uncomfortable compromise that unfortunately does serve as a symbol for our relationship as a whole.

This was not the worst story I have created during my years of activity, and yet I felt compelled to share this story as unlike the others which were more just kind of funny anecdotes to swap during a never-ending round of playing *I Never*, this had some very firm roots in the issue of fornicating flare-ups, and I feel very compelled to affirm that sometimes, a compromise is best. It will be worth it in the long run - delayed sex is infinitely better than abbreviated sex followed by a systematic pummelling from all other organs.

Lisa Cummins
My UC History

Hi, my name is Lisa Cummins, I'm 27 and I got diagnosed with ulcerative colitis at 18. I was still in secondary school.

A few weeks before I got my Christmas break I got a stomach bug and I was vomiting and had diarrhoea.

I went to A&E and the doctor in there gave me fluids and sent me home. That had past and I went back to school. So we finished up for Christmas.

A few days into the holiday I wasn't feeling great thinking the bug had come back but it was much worse; I couldn't eat or drink as I couldn't keep it down. I was throwing up bile.

I missed my Christmas dinner which I always look forward too. Thinking back now as I write this I don't remember much of Christmas week.

I was sleeping so much and I was constantly getting sick. My mam brought me up a drink called dioralyte to try help me keep up my fluids but I kept bringing it back up.

Then one day my mam came in to check on me and couldn't wake me. My aunt was over visiting and my mam called her and my dad and immediately took me into the hospital.

I don't remember the first few days in there as I was in and out of consciousness. I wasn't put on a ward for a while I was left on a trolley in a plaster room. Both my parents were always by my side taking it in turns.

I don't remember what was going on and I still don't to this day it's all a blur. I was told that the doctors had given me loads of IV fluids and steroids and antibiotics.

They had given me a camera test and I was so inflamed in my intestines they didn't want to operate as they said I was so young and wanted to try IV things first and lucky it worked and I kept my bowel.

They said if I had of came24hrs later they would have had to remove it.

I was in hospital for a month.

I had loads of tests done and X-rays and they told me I had UC. For the next few months I was on a liquid diet of yummy fortisips. Yuck. Because I was in bed for so long I hadn't used any of my muscles and I had to try walk again which was hard for me.

Eventually I was allowed to start on food I was so scared to start eating. I was crying as I was afraid I'd get sick again it was so difficult. But I managed to do it and I got home.

I had lost so much weight i was wearing size 12 clothes and now I was into 6. I was down to 6and a half stone. I was put on a medication called pentasa for my UC and I also found out I was anaemic so was put on iron tablets for that. But I had to have an iron infusion, Plus my periods had stopped for over a year too.

A few years later, before my 21st birthday, I got sick again and had the same symptoms and thought it was a flare up. But I had caught C diff.

I was kept in hospital for 2 weeks. I was then put on a medication called immuran.

When I was 23 I got a skin condition on my right foot called pyoderma. It caused my foot to swell, go red and get very hot and I couldn't walk. It was like my skin was dissolving I ended up with a hole on the side of my foot. Luckily the doctors managed to control it with antibiotics and steroids.

Then at 25 I had a abssess near my back passage and I had to go to A&E with that and they operated on it and I was kept in for three days.

At this point I was out of work. A month later I was back in hospital with swelling and bruising on my left leg it was red hot.

I was kept in for 4days and they said I had erathema nerdosa they gave me steroids and it had gone away and I was let home.

I'm now 27 I was taken off the immuran in January as I was told only allowed on it for five years. I was suffering with lower back pain and swelled right knee and stiff joints.

I was put on humria injection which is a biological.

So far so 4 months in it's helping me. I'm back eating the stuff I had to stop eating and I'm going the loo less now. I'm also back up to a healthy weight, So fingers crossed it stays that way. I was always In and out of work over the years as I was so sick.

I have since graduated college and I'm now a Montessori teacher and I have taken up dancing again. I couldn't have gotten through this without the help, love and support of family. It's been tough on us all but we are a strong close family who I love so much.

Thank you for taking the time to read my story. X

5.
Bad Company

Skipping ahead another few months from this and I had moved out. It was a dickish move on my part, whilst also being contradictorily one of my kindest gestures. My best friend at the time had just been left a house on his own, as well as a smattering of bills to try and cover with no job to speak of. We had already had the obligatory talks of how we should totally move in together bro, and I had already been putting aside money from the job I had just recently been made redundant for (due to an expired contract as opposed to anything at fault), so whilst not ideal I felt an obligation to help a friend in need. We had discussed it, albeit in a manner befitting of a serial show's recap rather than any true financial discourse, and myself and another friend would all move in together and between us, we could balance the bills in our own full fledged communist regime. After maybe a few hours of talk, I walked home, flung my bag into my still horrifically ordained bedroom and headed straight down to tell my mum the news. In one week's time the bathroom would be a safer environment.

What I find most perplexing about this period is that, although sprints to the bathroom were still frequent (as were the tears and painings) there was no spike in frequency. If anything they felt calmer. Maybe that cliché sense of rebellion and freedom of no longer living under a parent's rules and now making my own system with my friends was liberating to my intestinal tract, or a coincidence - I lose track sometimes.

The communist party fell just three months down the line, as once again it only looked really good when verbalised and not actually in action - splitting everything perfectly in threes including meals, and the various maintenance duties meant some people took favourites and one in particular flaunted every rule he could when came to washing, or universal foods. Tensions were high, not least because I had been currently sharing a room with the culprit and trying to juggle his ignorance for privacy with a budding relationship communicating our various lustings through the powerful 2.3 mega pixels and lag, afforded to us by a Tesco Value webcam and a lagging Skype connection. We had received a letter through the post from the council informing us we had three months to vacate the premises that one of us at least had lived in all of his life because we had been found unsuitable for it. This was not because it was a two bedroom residence with three individuals having to share, no, this was because during their stay my friend's mother had become disabled and so customised some aspects to help with her day to day life, and so now it was to be declared solely for disabled people which none of us fit the billing. After briefly debating breaking some legs (tensions were high as I say!) we settled that this was technically fair from a certain viewpoint, just not great for us, and set about trying to move.

Within a month a place was found, and I was brought to it as a deciding vote, and despite voicing my hatred of the place and everything about it from the boggy stains along the window sills, to the fact my bedroom would now be so small that it would be only fractionally larger than my smallest bedroom of my toddler years. I was reassured this would only be a temporary stay so we had a fallback whilst looked for a real place to settle on and so grudgingly, not wanting to be a letdown for my friends, I thought I could brave discomfort and having almost the entirety of my possessions and furniture dominating the lounge space for a few months. We signed the lease and moved in in the summer of 2008. I moved out July 2013.

The area itself we soon found out, had the highest crime rate in the entirety of the Wigan area, and that made itself abundantly clear when in one single day we were robbed no less than five times; three of which were whilst the police were here investigating the initial act. As time passed and my friendship with my roommates reached a breaking point, they moved away at varying intervals and I found myself living with my girlfriend of the time, known almost universally as Cretin. By this time I had already lost my life savings and all other forms of short change I had tried to amass during my time, but gained a relatively steady job that comfortably covered me as I tried to support myself and my girlfriend, who had been vehemently pushing the idea that she was agoraphobic. Naturally this put her on sickness benefits, and I became her sort of carer - though she saw fit to never fill in the relevant forms to make this any financial benefit to me.

We also started to receive frequent visits from our neighbours downstairs, who would start punching into the wood of our door until we creaked it open, at which point they would threaten to strangle, maim, and outright murder us if we did not stop the racket we had been apparently guilty of. Indeed, we were known to turn the pages of our respective books with a thunderclap that shook the walls to its very core. Not always feeling brave enough for sarcasm, I often just let him rally off all of the activities we were supposedly guilty of; most notably sex despite always being able to the answer the door fully dressed, bone dry, and notably boneless, with relative speed. There was a time where the mistake was made of contacting the police, but this simply encouraged the matter as they could only be told complaints had been made and then left to their own devices, this merely empowered the crazed drug-addled lunacy.

It will come to no surprise to any sufferer, or indeed reader who has been with me up to this point, that this had a notable effect on my intestinal tract. If there is one thing I could ever vouch for Cretin (whose name will become apparent in time) it was that she did do her best to try and not just live with my mystery illness, but actively supported it. In fact during the first year with her, the effects showed a notably decline in frequency and although I still had huge brackets of the food world cordoned off for safety to me, it was becoming just one-to-two incidents a week instead of a nightly pain. Unless of course we had been particularly aggressively reading that week requiring extra visitations from the Jeremy Kyle famers.

As the summer slowly started to cool down

(which in England terms means the next day it was fucking freezing), Cretin was busy casually monitoring the dark corners of the internet, headphones thankfully locking away the commonplace screams of some of the animations, and I was sat on the other end of our king-sized bed adopting the more innocent side with Facebook. An inbox message popped up - this being obviously not uncommon in itself, so clicked curiously to find a greeting from Amy. Amy was a girl who had been my best friend after an unfortunate house party I had been privy to, in which we both made friends out of our own social ineptitude with those around us, which led to a year realising how much we shared in common, and so when her boyfriend would come to visit my roommate, Amy and I would often go to another room to do our own thing instead. However we had lost contact for a long time by this point, so this came as something of shock and a lurch pulled at my stomach as a years worth of emotions and memories came flooding through every pore of my body. The sudden gushing brought about a faint sick feeling, and my ever-analytical mind started trying to run through a game of connecting the dots that a simple "hey, long time no speak" message could bring and it was some minutes before I mustered enough in me to be able to even respond. I had been completely unsure as to why we had lost contact and so felt at this point I had maybe given off some wrong vibes to her, and of course was not something I could have broached to her - I may not be the height of social autonomy, but I know "so how are you?" should never be followed by "why did we stop talking?".

So we began talking on Facebook for a little while, and I found myself feeling a sense of butterflies when I would now see that same dullard inbox notification pop up knowing it was another little titbit from her. We began moving this to texting, almost immediately at an incessant volume meaning our first month of contact left with a nearly £70 charge on my phone bill which was offering 300 free texts. But we were having such fun texting absolutely inane banter that to anyone else would seem pointless, but to us was some crucial information of our day, or just amusing anecdote, and so I took to paying to upgrade my phone contract to allow for unlimited texts to cover these spam sessions.

This budding friendship obviously caught the attention of the Cretin I was currently living alongside, which took her once supportive side and began to warp it into a spiteful beast. I had made the mistake of showing her a couple of vulnerabilities, and she began sitting on them with all of her increasing body mass in the desperate hopes that I wouldn't run off with Amy. Though this didn't affect my bowels as much, this did give me a serious drain of any morale I had been working to boost for myself and spent some days feeling so pathetic with myself, that I could barely muster the strength to leave for long periods of the day. Cretin had been working hard to isolate me from a large portion of my friends, and now I had managed to bring one back into my life who brought out a better side to me than she could, it turned her miserable husk into the form of a flatulating Hulk.

The Cretin had turned from a woman I would declare a love for, to my own worst enemy (outside of myself of course), and as this escalated Amy and I became closer still, and to this day she is regarded as the single best friend I could have ever hoped for. And for many months that followed the sole thing to keep me from a complete and utter depression crushing me completely, and I owe her everything for that.

The Life and Times of Rebecca Crawford

I'm Rebecca Crawford, 19 from North Ayrshire, Scotland.

Shortly after New Year 2013, I started experiencing pains in my stomach and feeling really tired all the time. I was also finding blood whenever I went to the toilet(which was a lot more than normal). I found this extremely scary and embarrassing and so I kept it to myself. However, my mum noticed that something was not quite right with me but I just kept saying "I'm fine!". The last thing I wanted was to admit that this embarrassing thing was happening to me! It just wasn't something you talk about.

There was one day, a few weeks after that I was visiting family with my boyfriend and I had to go the toilet...again there was blood. I knew this couldn't go on any longer, I had also been losing a lot of weight and not eating properly. This was the day that I took a step in looking after my health. I told my boyfriend of 8 months everything that had been going on, it was not an easy thing to do. Who wants to tell their BOYFRIEND something as embarrassing as this!? However, he was so understanding and stressed to me that I had to see a doctor immediately! I told my mum when I got home, which I should have done much earlier on!

The next day I made an appointment to see a doctor and my boyfriend came with me. It was so horrible, I had to get an examination to see what was happening and have bloods taken. It was then decided that I would need to be referred to the hospital to get a camera test(colonoscopy). I was absolutely terrified at the thought!

So a few months later, in May 2013, after many doctors appointments and feeling so ill, my appointment letter came through from the hospital. It was the end of May when I went in for the procedure. My mum came with me but had to leave and was told to pick me up later. I was sedated which felt so strange but I watched the camera on the screen, seeing my insides. It was the strangest experience ever! Afterwards, I was allowed food and to go home. I went home and slept for the rest of the day.

I then got a follow up appointment in which my whole life changed forever. I was diagnosed with Ulcerative Colitis, a form of Inflammatory Bowel Disease, something I had never even heard of! I thought it would be something I could just take some pills for and be back to normal in no time. God, was I wrong! When I was told there was no cure and that I would have it for life, I felt numb.

So I was given medication to help the inflammation in my colon stay in control and sent away to try and come to terms with now having a long-term illness. The months following my diagnosis are a bit of a blur as I tried to adjust to this news. I went on holiday with friends, got engaged and moved in with my new fiancé. I was just trying to lead a normal life and I started feeling a bit better.

In October 2013, I had my first flare-up. I had never felt so ill in my life! I was being sick, going to the toilet so many times a day, not eating and feeling so weak I could hardly walk. Not to mention the pain! Every single morning for weeks, I would wake up with agonizing stomach pains and it was terrifying. I had to take a lot of time off work and college and was basically bed-ridden. It got so bad that I called NHS 24 and they told me to go see a doctor. I had to go to an on-call doctor as it was the weekend and he gave me Imodium to settle my stomach. When I got home I realised that on the label it said "Don't take if you have Ulcerative Colitis", but I assumed that the doctor knew what he was talking about and it would help me.

The next evening, I was in severe pain, not eating and vomiting all the time. I phoned my mum for help and passed out from the pain. Luckily my fiancé was with me and he called an ambulance. I got rushed straight to A&E and was given anti-sickness medication which I took a really bad reaction to; my heart was beating out of my chest and the room was spinning. I don't really remember much else from being in A&E, just that I had to get an X-ray and blood taken. I also had to be given fluids through a drip as I was severely dehydrated. I was kept in and had to stay in for 5 days, during which I received another colonoscopy and had to have an iron infusion of 3 bags of blood as I was severely anaemic. It was hell being in the hospital but I knew it was for the best. After the five days were up, I felt so much better, had more energy and was eating and drinking again.

August 2014.

Now, over a year since my diagnosis, I was in remission for a couple of months but I started flaring up a few weeks ago. The only symptoms I had were pain, tiredness and nausea. I went to the doctors and was told to use foam enemas and take iron pills. However, after a couple of weeks on these the pain was getting worse and so I began taking co-codamol. I am recently out of hospital for the second time as I was in excruciating pain and had to be taken in. I was told it was due to the co-codamol and the iron pills bunging me up. I was discharged after staying overnight but I have now been taken of my medication and waiting for an appointment with my Gastro-Intestinal doctor to do some tests.

Life is very different for me now, I don't take things for granted like I used to. However, there have been some negative things to this disease apart from the obvious!...I don't go out with friends often and feel as if some of them don't get it or understand, it makes me isolated because I'm a teenager and should be out enjoying myself instead of being stuck at home feeling ill.I have my bad day and my good days, there are days when it really gets me down.I am definitely trying to stay positive though and I couldn't do it without my wonderful family and my fiancé who have been by my side the whole way!

A few weeks ago, I joined the amazing support group on Facebook, #GetYourBellyOut. Everyone on there is so supportive and made me realise that I am not alone! I am so grateful to be a part of it and hope in the future that I can help raise more awareness for Inflammatory Bowel Disease!

6.
New Endings and Old Beginnings

This year marked the tenth anniversary of the day my life changed forever.
2014 brought about a great number of changes, and I was now moving from a comfortable financial place to being threatened with a constant stream of life on the streets. Every day seemed to signal another letter, and if I made it through the front door without that ominous gentle thud of an envelope then I would face the violent shredding of *Rock You Like A Hurricane* from my phone with something worse.

My depression was back, and had hit a serious peak. The obvious lull of facing simultaneous anniversaries of death, the move, and of course the day my constant lust for food became trial by fire, was also now being met with a three hour a week job leaning to a dependency on the dole that would have an obvious dip in morale. The hours of my job had dropped so dramatically due to a 'temporary' relocation so that the company would not have to pay compensation for the period of my previous residence coming to an end. I was set on a shelf like a damaged toy, my superiors in a constant flux of "I'll do it this afternoon" without my ever entering their memory furthermore.

The interaction with the council led to more than a dozen letters summoning me to court for bills that had been paid, or in no less than seven cases bills that were paid, and then after call for an investigation, it had been discovered should never have been paid at all. Which of course meant I would be refunded… one sixth of what had been paid.

I mention all this, not to whine or try and broach sympathy, but to summise the events that transpired one after the other to bring it all back. May 2014, after over one year of a nice tranquil life of no sightings of trouble (of course still second and triple guessing every meal and drink I would consume) my bowels hit back. And they hit back hard.

I was back at college, using the opportunity of reduced hours to improve on my CV to ensure a career where this would not repeat itself. The majority of lessons I found myself breaking into halves with toilet intervals, some of which became false alarms leading to a rather embarrassingly short return to classroom, and others dominated some lessons. This itself was increasingly manageable, albeit tiresome, with increasing comfort brought from a new group of friends one of whom became a very strong inspiration. She suffered very notably from Crohn's disease, and although it had taken a toll on her, she elevated above it with such a grace and ease had she never warned in advance, I'd have struggled on most days to even know she was sick. She was something to truly aspire to, and seeing her and knowing even on a surface level what she was fighting, made me definitely want to fight harder myself. I mean c'mon, I have done this dance for a full decade now, it was time to try and not dance around the incidents in a constant fear of embarrassing myself. Now was the time to just push the limits - I could eat two of these and feel my stomach come charging to beat me up for my lunch money?

Well then fuck you, I'll manage four because that's what I *want* to manage. If I could summise this level of rebellion in one expression, it would be taken straight from the character Willow's rebellious phase on the show *Buffy The Vampire Slayer* "And I'm eating this banana. Lunchtime be damned!"

As I have mentioned, my incidents had become increasingly sparse under the tyrannical rule of Cretin, but since Amy's return to my life and the eviction of the beast, my flare-ups had come to a complete halt. Even after the eviction of Cretin brought about some of the aforementioned court threats and excessive financial struggles, I had a fantastic calming influence now in my life. Though she of course is still there through every struggle, the rapid-fire succession of these problems meant stress still became very much a factor. Bleeding had returned by this time, and become more prevailant than before; what had been a special guest spot in my life had now been designated a main character.

I spent the next few months ignoring the obvious desire to visit a doctor about this. Why bother? I thought. The memory of that back alley visit still stung through the fibres of my being, and was tainting my own judgement. I'd had ten years experience afterall, I knew what I was doing! And if I had any questions, I know had a friend who knew of the suffering who could answer this.

It was only through the middle of April, when my friend had messaged me about her involvement in a Twitter takeover that any of this changed. She had tweeted an image of her belly from her first hospital visit and what it looked like as of now, as part of a trending event dubbed #GetYourBellyOut designed to raise awareness for IBD afflictions Ulcerative Colitis and Crohn's disease. I was really moved by this campaign, and though I was still at this time under the old assumption it would be IBS which is a very different beast, I just wanted to do my part to raise awareness for my amazing friend and do what little part I could for anyone else going through this.

It transpired that this trend came from a Facebook group that had just recently started to form, and I had now not only netted a few extra followers and retweets to boost my non-existent ego, but I had been offered an official invite to join. There was a strong sense of guilt and embarrassment at first; what right do I have? I don't even have a diagnosis! Who am I to complain in a group that is at first glance filled with stories far more traumatic than my own? For me to complain about a date night of me trying to woo my nearest bucket with a free meal, felt insignificant in comparison to someone who has gone so far as to have a stoma attached requiring a severed intestine. It's an expression I could never tolerate as a cultural theme, but the "first world problems" moniker felt appropriate to my own issues next to their own struggles.

I forced myself to post regardless, after all I hadn't just crashed the party, they had invited me. I may feel like a fraud, but maybe there is something to this? For a little while it still felt kind of wrong and though I would comment relatively frequently doing my best to offer a little helpful speech or lame anecdote to make someone's life even a little happier for that moment, I would not make a post about myself. But as the months blurred, I found myself establishing friends with the community and braved my first post and loved it. This isn't an ego thing, but it was beautiful to see me throw out something that I had struggled with for a decade and been completely alone throughout, and now I could talk about the more disgusting aspects of my life, and have some people joking and telling stories of how it happened to them too! I was beginning to feel normal for just once in my new life my move to Wigan had afforded me.

And so I stand here in the bathtub, my dressing gown dancing through the chilled breeze, revealing the jeans and shirt promising a walk out I was not capable of. But even though I'm currently craning my head through the bathroom window to catch every hint of the cool air I can to try and soothe the current war fighting through my lower intestines, I can't help but smile. True I've had a rocky time I don't think I'd wish on anyone, and despite a gap year giving me a taste of a normal life, I can't see it continuing. But I don't mind right now, because although this pain will never become something I'm used to and find anything other than a burden, I'm better now than I have ever been. I have managed to brave another appointment with a doctor thanks to the support from the group, and this time when my blood results came back compulsive liars, rather than just ignoring the conflicting information, my doctor pursued it and I am now left with a handful of Moviprep sachets to prepare me for the next step in getting a final diagnosis.

After ten years of waiting, I will finally get an answer to my problem, and that answer is Ulcerative Colitis. At least that's what the general verdict is through the community and specialist's currently finding ways to prove this suspicion. But the important part is, I'm still fighting this battle, but now I am not alone. I have an army beside me of my best friends, and the entirety of the #GetYourBellyOut community. And that is pretty damn special.

#GetYourBellyOut Story

....So Far

A poem by

Gemma Lester

I'm going to tell you a story,

so sit back and relax.

I promise it won't last forever,

but it's one you'll never forget.

Our story starts with four girl's,

with a story that needed to be told.

They had the strength and courage to tell it,

and new it had to be bold.

It's not just our heroines who suffer,

but people around the globe.

They wanted to help these people,

and show them their never alone.

#GetYourBellyOut was created,

on the night of April 3rd.

At 9.01 in the evening,

their voices started to be heard.

From all the corners of the world,

over 700 answered the call.

Everyone in the group agreed,

it was now time for a change.

And by a unanimous vote,

time for world domination was declared.

The girls put their heads together,

and said we mustn't hide.

So we pulled our shirts and jumpers up,

to show our scars with pride.

The wheels were now in motion,

our emotions running high.

But in true #GetYourBellyOut style,

we all stood united as one.

We pulled out our phones and started snapping

away,

'let's see your best belly shot'.

Our challenge was not done,

we still had a way to go,

our pictures we now must show.

Upload, Download, Facebook and then Tweet,

write a little of yourself,

press send and then repeat.

In no time at all,

our pictures were all there,

for the whole world to see and share.

The support we received was overwhelming,

our cries were being heard.

People took the time out to help us,

all their pictures and donations were amazing.

Never in our wildest dreams,

did we imagine this much support.

The girls were not done,

and a video was released,

our bellies now on the big screen.

The song was right,

it brought tears to my eyes,

a tissue now in both hands.

We congratulated the girls on a job well done,

and thanked them for all their hard work.

No longer were we hiding,

and no longer were we scared.

I was no longer keeping a secret,

it was out there for all to share.

I was now standing strong,

for the first time since I was 21.

Now word has spread,

the group has grown,

it gets bigger by the day.

We laugh, we cry, we sing and dance,

we help each other through the day.

We talk of poop and bags and things,

stomas by the score.

Crohn's, Colitis, IBD,

we hope there will one day be a cure.

No one is ever left behind,

Listening is what we do.

No walking away or being left alone,

even if we're on the loo.

We send cyber hugs and kisses,

when someone's having a crappy day.

we're always there to listen,

no matter what time of day.

We owe you girls oh so much,

we know that life is tough,

and sometimes we don't say it,

because words are just not enough.

We're all insane, even a little mad,

we have our quirky little ways.

Where else can everyone here say,

Fridays is #toiletselfie day.

Again it's you girls we have to thank,

for bringing us all together.

Who knows what's next,

and what's up your sleeves,

but something tells me it will be rather crazy.

Whatever it is, we will make it succeed,

and make you girls so proud.

I'm sorry to say, I've come to the end,

It's now time for me to say bye bye.

I'm sorry to go,

it won't be for long,

part 2 is already on its way.

But before I go, I would just like to say,

Thank you for what you have achieved.

But most of all, I would like to say,

thank you for our new big family.

I know the other bellies are just as proud,

and would want to say,

you make us all so proud

THE END..........FOR NOW :-)

Victoria Marie
Colitis & Me - A Tale From A #GetYourBellOut Founder

When you're young you don't think about being sick, you think it only happens in later life. You go day to day working too hard, partying a bit much and shopping until you drop. I was enjoying a hectic life running from one job to the next, one party to the after party, one sleep over with the girls to the next. I was 21, beginning to travel to different places and starting to figure out who I was as a person and finding my feet. I was beginning to feel comfortable within my own skin, just setting out in life. Then all of a sudden all I had ever known came to a stop and everything I had ever known came crashing down around my ears. Something happened that meant never again would I be the person I was only just starting to get to know.

Almost five years ago now I got diagnosed with Ulcerative Colitis and it changed my entire world. All that you thought you knew about life – forget it. All those plans you have in your calender – clear them. All you thought you had planned out on the table – forget it all. Life is about to change forever, and no you get no say in it at all!!

You might have heard about Crohn's Disease or Ulcerative Colitis in the news recently so here is a little more about it and first hand experience of my journey with Ulcerative Colitis.

Ulcerative Colitis and Crohn's Disease mean there is an imbalance of bacteria in our guts/colons. In the average person there is 'good bacteria' fighting off the 'bad bacteria'. When it comes to those with the illness it means our good bacteria is working over time and trying to fight off an infection (the bad bacteria) which does not even exist. So instead of attacking the bad bacteria, it attacks the wall of our colon instead. This leads to inflammation and ulcers, cramps and pain.

Main symptoms just to get you up to speed are vomiting, Anemia, more trips to the loo, loss of appetite, weight-loss, swollen joints and many more. Not to mention all of the secondary symptoms from medications and problems caused by taking these long term. Alongside these there are things like stress, anxiety, Iron deficiency, depression etc, the list is endless! This results in extensive trial and error to find a medication to soothe the symptoms. Some unfortunate souls end up having to have serious invasive surgery to avoid blockages, ruptures and all sorts of complications. There are far too many now living without parts of their colons/intestines.

I started nipping back and forth from the bathroom, I didn't think anything more of it. I just assumed I had an upset stomach. I was too afraid and highly embarrassed to talk about it so I simply stuck my head in the sand and did nothing about it. BIG MISTAKE! I left it – I just ran back and forth to the bathroom all day and night. I threw up continuously, suffered numerous fevers and had no appetite though I was starving inside. I shoved my head under the duvet, where I spent every day too weak to move thinking I was dyeing. In the end I was 6 stone thin and bones when I EVENTUALLY checked myself into hospital. By then sleeping on pillows with one wedged between my knees became the norm just to try and find comfort. I was passed the point of dehydration and exhaustion when I rolled myself into A&E, I jammed my body between the chairs in the waiting room because my head felt like a boulder. I can't imagine how terrified my mother must have been to watch me deteriorate in such a horrible way and that is one of my biggest regrets. To have put her through so much torture as she watched day by day pleading with me to get checked out. I waited a whole year – what an idiot!! A whole year because I couldn't muster the courage to talk about it.

That was back in 2009 and since then life has never been the same. My illness has taken away everything I knew, I have been through the ringer and am not yet sure I have come out the other side. My illness is invisible to the unsuspecting public which is where a lot of frustration and lack of understanding comes from. Just because a person does not appear to be sick, please do not assume that all is well. "But you don't look sick" is often the sentence that gets banded around which is totally unhelpful.

I used to be care free I came and went as I chose. Now my days are filled with anxiety and worry. I can't make plans with friends or family for not want of letting them down. My illness is really unreliable so I often have to cancel plans, this causes much friction and frustration. I can spend weeks looking forward to an event/outing only for my tummy to play up the night before and ruin all my plans. Gone is the care free spirit who could pack her case and head in any direction she so chose. All of the simple pleasures I once enjoyed now seem so far out of reach. I struggle to hold down a job as employers are oblivious to the seriousness of these illnesses, where once was the hard working dependable staff member now is a person who feel a burden and out of place. Gone in the work-a-holic and in its place is the chronic fatigue young adult who I sometimes fail to recognize.

What do I wish people knew about my illness? That to date there is no cure, I have an illness that will forever be at my side. Though I may laugh and smile I am dealing with more than any young person should have to deal with. Imagine your intestines being covered in ulcers and having food pass by them each day of your life, painful right? Simply because you see me out in the public does not mean I am feeling great, sufferers tend to put on a brave performance and will rarely let you in on the true extent of how we are really feeling.

Some people react to their diagnosis with the attitude 'This illness will not beat me' and they find some super human strength to scale mountains and achieve their every goal. But it is important too to remember that for some, simply fighting such a life altering illness can be hard enough without pushing themselves to the brink.

Aside from those marathon runners and rising stars there are those who are confined to the house too worries, afraid and exhausted to do much more than get dressed in the mornings. Both Crohn's Disease and Ulcerative Colitis are unique to each individual person, there is no one size fits all and there is no manual on how to cope with IBD.

Despite all of this, underneath I am still the same emerging soul that I once was. Only now I am stronger in every way imaginable. I went for years without talking to a single other person who has Ulcerative Colitis or Crohn's Disease. Therefore back in December of 2013 I started a blog and 'Colitis and ME' was born. I have never made a better decision in my life!! Creating my blog opened up a whole new world that I never knew existed. I began by talking about my journey with my illness and in flooded the messages from people who are going through the exact same troubles as I am. I can't begin to explain the amount of comfort and support that comes from talking to another individual who is in your shoes.

A few things you should know:

Both Ulcerative Colitis and Crohn's Disease are VERY serious illnesses which is always frustrating when the media play down the impact it can have on peoples lives.

Both Crohn's and Colitis fall into an umbrella known as Inflammatory Bowel Disease (IBD) which is commonly confused with (Irritable bowel syndrome) IBS.

There are over 5 million people world wide who suffer every single day. Unlike the flu it is an illness which is with us every second of every day and is involved in every choice we make. It is safe to say that Colitis has become my shadow try as I might to ignore it.

They are still unsure what the cause is as each case is unique to the individual. Many have surgery to prevent worsening illness and in some cases life saving surgery but as of yet there is NO CURE.

There is a whole team working behind the scenes to try and get more awareness of this horrible disease. There are advocates running marathons, rowing the Atlantic, organizing charity balls and so forth all in a bid to raise much needed funds to put towards research. There is so much hope that one day we will all get the cure we all so desperately deserve, to prevent young children having to suffer and to give others a break from the relentlessness of Ulcerative Colitis and Crohn's Disease.

Many don't like to talk about it and I can whole heatedly understand why. To discuss running back and forth to the bathroom all day is not something people want to talk about. Those who suffer with Ulcerative Colitis and Crohn's Disease develop a super human strength, they battle on and take every knock after knock. These illnesses are very unpredictable and it is time they were taken seriously. What I would like more than anything is for people to be educated about both Ulcerative Colitis and Crohn's Disease, so that we can live in a world which has a little more kindness and understanding to those already suffering a great deal at the hands of our illness without having to deal with the burden of judgement.

Take a walk in my shoes, I guarantee it will change you in every way imaginable.

With love, Victoria Marie of 'Colitis and ME'

To hear more please join me over on my blog www.colitisandme.blogspot.co.uk where you can contact me from there. I look forward to hearing from you all x

We Have Guts! (They're Just Defective)

A poem by
Alex Monk

We fight a war you cannot see.

We don't always bare our scars for all to see.

Each battle we fight in our endless war from inside can last for hours, days, weeks or years.

We never give up, we stand strong and fight on in this silent, lonely, hidden war.

It seems never ending and we just want a break!

It's hard to see the light sometimes, when the darkness is all around but we never stop fighting to find the bright white light that we know is there somewhere.

The fighting is hard, it's tiring, lonely, it drains our

energy and makes us feel weak, it holds us back from the path we wish to take but we fight on in our search to find our way back.

Why oh why do we fight on??

We fight on because we're strong, we can rest our tired bodies until we can stand up tall and carry on again.

We have friends and family to bring us laughter, a smile, or a simple hug to drive the loneliness away.

But most of all we have the heart and strength of a Spartan warrior. We will never give up and we will never surrender.

Be strong my friends, fight on, you're not alone anymore.

Lorna Haymes
Holiday Checklist & Flying For Ostomates

I'm on my 2nd stoma/ileostomy, however I was scared of traveling abroad with the first one so I gave it a miss. This time Eve (aka my ilesostomy) is here to stay and I for one WILL NOT be staying in rainy Manchester when the beaches of the world are screaming my name… lorrnnna come and lay your pastey white body on my soft golden sands….

So I've had to figure out whats what and it seems like prepare well in advance seems to be the key message from support sites and people I've spoken too.

So one of the first things I'd look at is travel insurance. If you don't have insurance with an stoma you could leave yourself in a whole host of trouble if anything happens abroad. Its essential that ostomates ensure that the level of travel insurance cover is sufficient. All your medical history, surgery and pre-existing conditions (including stomas), must be disclosed to the travel insurance company. Otherwise the travel insurance may be invalid, and they could refuse to pay if you need to claim. Please make sure that the travel insurance company confirms in writing that cover is provided for ALL your pre-existing medical conditions, including a stoma. Read the policy's small print, e.g. level of cover, any excess payments required on making a claim, any age limits applied, exclusions, etc. The chances of you needing to contact your insurance company whilst on holiday or small, but you don't want to be stuck thinking your covered for your stoma or your IBD when actually that one teeny tiny line at the end of the terms and conditions says haha we have took your money but wont actually help you!!

If your from the UK and travelling to a European Economic Area (EEA) country, it is essential to obtain a European Health Insurance Card (EHIC). The EHIC replaces the prevoius E111 form. In most European countries, this card entitles you to reduced or sometimes free medical treatment, if treatment is unfortunatlky needed during your holiday.

The card is only valid for treatment offered under the state healthcare schemes operating in these countries, it gives access to treatment under the same terms as people who live in the destination country.

Countries currently in the EEA are Austria, Belgium, Bulgaria, Cyprus, Czech Republic, Denmark, Estonia, Finland, France, Germany, Greece, Hungary, Iceland, Ireland, Italy, Latvia, Liechtenstein, Lithuania, Luxembourg, Malta, Netherlands, Norway, Poland, Portugal, Romania, Slovakia, Slovenia, Spain, Sweden and Switzerland.

The EHIC is definitely not a replacement for getting travel insurance. Like I said before travel insurance is essential!!

You can get an application form for the EHIC and a booklet at large post offices which includes a full list of countries covered and details of their health systems, the booklet is called 'Health Advice For Travellers'

The telephone number from the UK to phone for more information about the EHIC is 0845 606 2030, or go to the following website. http://www.nhs.uk/NHSEngland/Healthcareabroad/EHIC/Pages/about-the-ehic.aspx

Now the bit I love the packing of the case…. this is where I always realise just how many clothes I've bought "ooh that would be nice for holiday" or "I will save that till my holiday" I lay it all out on my bed and pray to the suitcase gods that it all fits in. Needless to say I worried that I might have to curb my spending pre holiday until I found out that I can put all my ostomy products in my hand luggage. My stoma nurse advised me to pack all my stoma appliances/equipment in clear plastic bags (e.g. freezer or sandwich bags), so that they aren't as bulky as when they are in the boxes. Ive been advised to put a supply of ostomy products in each bag that I'm taking. She said if I'm going for two weeks then put a two week supply in my hand luggage and a two week supply in my partners hand luggage, and to have a back up supply of ostomy products in my case then if the worst happens, we loose one of our bags, I will have a decent supply for traveling. She told me to always take double the amount of ostomy supplies I'd need for the trip incase of unforeseen circumstances ie the ash cloud that grounded flights for weeks a few years back. Taking double your ostomy suppies will also stop any worry of running out so you can relax on holiday knowing that you have more than enough for the trip.

If you've packed all ostomy supplies in clear bags in your hand luggage, when you arrives at security, if the luggage is searched, then the ostomy products are clearly visible to the security staff and you don't have to drag everything out. It can also be handy to have a copy of a prescription in the bags to show that they are medical supplies.

If you have the correct medical documentation then there is no reason why you cannot take all your ostomy products including your adhesive removal sprays on the plane in your hand luggage barring sisscors. I would also make sure you have some spare adhesive removal sprays in your case just incase you catch security staff on an "off" day (I'd also recommend you take some of the adhesive removal wipes just to be on the safe side)

Please look at this link for hand luggage restrictions paying attention to section 4 about medical supplies https://www.gov.uk/hand-luggage-restrictions/overview

So your though the baggage bit and now for the x-ray machine for you and your hand luggage… your ostomy bag and supplies will show up on these machines and the staff may want to search you or your hand luggage. To stop any issues you can carry a travel certificate. Its a pocket-sized, multi-lingual travel certificate and can prove very useful. This certificate states in different languages that you have a medical condition.

The certificate explains the necessary medical supplies being carried and that they must be with you at all times, and that you, the stoma patient, requires a private room, with a qualified physician in attendance, should a search be necessary. Obviously, this travel certificate can be extremely useful to facilitate passing through security and customs with your medical equipment at airports, and also in case of a body search, which are becoming more common these days. If a pouch or any ostomy equipment is selected for a search, it is best to ask if the content could be viewed 'somewhere less public'. Hopefully, airport security will respect your privacy.

It is advisable to keep the travel certificate (and the letter from your doctor) in your pocket, so if needed your able to explain your medical condition, whilst keeping it discreet.

Depending on the issuing company of the travel certificate, languages available are Arabic, Chinese, Croatian, English, French, German, Greek, Hindi, Italian, Mandarin, Middle East,

Polish, Portuguese, Punjabi, Russian, Spanish, Thai, Turkish and Vietnamese. Some of the companies and associations, who offer these travel certificates free to any ostomate on request, are:

http://www.dansac.co.uk/default.asp?Action=Details&Item=189

http://www.colostomyassociation.org.uk/

http://www.iasupport.org/faq/national-office-faqs

http://www.securicaremedical.co.uk/Menu/Lifestyle-Tips/Travel.aspx

Your stoma nurse should also be able to help you with travel cards/certificates but please make sure you ask well in advance of your holiday so you know if they have access to them or not.

So you've passed all the tests, your through security, your suitcase has been wizzed off down that chute at the back of the check in agent, you've walked through duty free 3 times, sprayed every single perfume or aftershave so much that your wrist now smells of that many different perfumes you have no idea which one is which. You've been shocked at the prices they want to charge you for a simple sandwich but hey you pay it anyway, by this point you just want a sit down with a bite to eat and a drink… then you hear it your flight is being called woopieeee suntan here I come….

On the flight if you need to use a toilet, try to go when there are no trolleys blocking the isle and before the meal is served, there will be fewer queues than after.

Making a separate, small travel kit can make trips to the toilet discreet and uncomplicated. Similar to my hand bag kit in my youtube video

Some ostomates prefer a larger capacity pouch for long flights, or for when pouch changes/emptying could be delayed.

When flying don't be alarmed if your pouch balloons a little with wind. It is not known exactly why this happens, but it could be due to altitude, not being able to exercise, change of normal eating patterns or change in cabin pressure. If needs be just take yourself off to the bathroom to empty and release the air. I've had a look online and some advice to try and ease the extra wind is as follows: before and during the flight try and limit or refrain from having fizzy drinks, alcohol, and fried, fatty or spicy foods. If you let the fizzy drinks to go flat first this will help reduce wind. In addition, it is better to eat sensibly and regularly for the 24 hours before the flight, and avoid any food or drink that is known to cause wind.

As per the norm, it's recommended by all airlines to do leg exercises, walk around the aircraft cabin at least once an hour, and drink plenty of water.

So that's it for this blog however I will be doing a blog soon with hint and tips for when your on your holiday.

I hope by me putting this information together then it makes life a little easier so your not searching the interweb loosing the will to live.

Thanks for your time love and hugs Lorna....

Enjoy your holidays!!!!!!

Posted in Uncategorized on June 16, 2014. Leave a comment

STEROIDS..DUN DUN DERRRRRR

Hi everyone its me again, hope your all well... I thought I'd do another blog as I seem to have caught the buzz. I love watching the counter going up knowing that people are reading and I hope that it might just help one of you readers....

if that's you then yay my hard work is paying off.

Please feel free to post a comment below regarding my blog or requests for things that you would like me to cover.

So I best get on with it today I'm going to talk about steroids… ARRRHHH

Yes we all do it as soon as the DR says… "I think a short course of steroids will calm down this inflammation"… NOOOOOOOO!!! Weight gain, sleepless nights, sweating, mood swings, taking up residence in the kitchen mainly with head in the fridge. I don't know about you lot but I have three sets of clothes in my wardrobe… ill clothes for when I loose a lot of weight, healthy clothes and larger clothes for the steroid weight gain.

steroid 3

I for one have never been on a short course of

steroids its always over a month... DRS THIS IS NOT MY IDEA OF SHORT.

I've been on 3 different types of oral steroids since being diagnosed with IBD 12 years ago. I will go in to each of them individually and how I got on with them.

Im going to call the steroids by the brand names I've been given by my gastro Dr;

Budesonide: These are what they give me when I have mild inflammation. A quick fix hopefully to nip the little bugger into order. Generally I'm put on a high dose. I don't seem to have any side effects with these ones, however they also don't seem to effect my inflammation at all. Drs have come to the conclusion its just not worth giving me budesonide anymore as I always end up on the more potent steroids in the end.. Its just a waste of time for me and it gives my inflammation chance to get worse whilst I'm on them.

Prednisolone: I've been on these more times than I care to remember as im sure most of you reading this have too… these are the ones I dread having. I usually start on a high dose between 40mg and 60mgs depending on how bad I am at the time. I swear as soon as these get put in my hand at the chemist I get hungry and my backside expands!! These are the ones that give me night sweats, sleepless nights, constant craving of food and very moody (I mean stay about a mile away and agree with everything I say or I may erupt) I tend to cry a lot to but unsure if this is the tablets or the fact that I'm probably quite ill by this point. I hold a lot of water too which makes me bloat and get the infamous "moonface" A nurse once told me if you limit your salt intake then it should help ease a bit of the swelling, however trying to tell my head "step away from the crisps" never works. Despite all this these tablets really work on calming my flares down at high doses, however sometimes I have to go back up when I'm weaning cause my flare gets a little cocky and doesn't do as its told. I always make sure I take some kind of protection for my stomach too either omeprazole or lansoprazole.

Deflazacort: I have been given these as unfortunately I was accidently given 100mg overdose of prednisolone for 11 days after an operation which caused me to have steroid induced psychosis therefore I can no longer have these tablets as my body reacts very badly even at a 20mg dose. Anywho so I now have these. They come in 6mg tablets rather than 5mg like the two above. You take them the same as the other two ie first thing in the morning to mimic your bodies natural cycle. I found that these do give me some of the same side effects as the prednisolone, moonface, night sweats food cravings . The mood swings didn't seem as bad for me though but that might not be the same for everyone These don't tend to work fantastic for me at a low dose but on a higher dose of 48mg they work just as well as the prednisolone.

This next paragraph is for safety reasons, I'm sure most of you are aware however it would be very irresponsible of me to do a blog on steroids without mentioning it:-

You must not stop taking steroids suddenly if you have been taking them for more than three weeks. This is because long-term use of corticosteroids can suppress the natural production of corticosteroids by the adrenal glands, which means that the body becomes temporarily reliant on the medicine. When it is time to stop treatment the dose should be tapered down gradually, to allow the adrenal glands to start producing adequate amounts of natural steroids again. Follow the instructions given by your doctor or pharmacist. Your doctor may also want you to stop treatment gradually if you have been taking high doses (more than 48mg deflazacort daily) even if only for three weeks or less; if you have been treated with corticosteroid tablets or injections in the last year; if you had problems with your adrenal glands before treatment was started; or if you have been repeatedly taking doses in the evening. (piece taken from netdoctor.co.uk)

On our #GetYourBellyOut facebook forum there are lots of people doing steroid face pictures and comparing them with their normal faces. It very interesting to see how different people can look. click and add yourself to the group to join in or find support and friends

https://www.facebook.com/groups/GetYourBellyOut/

During my time campaigning with #GetYourBellyOut its become clear that people aren't aware that there is a few different types of Crohns disease so here is a little blog roughly explaining which is which. I have the Terminal ileal type. Ive also been told I have colonic, however I would have thought if I had both it would be called Ileocolic... confused yeah me too but apparently as I have the joint pains and skin lesions I fall in to the separate boxes. Sometimes it best to just leave them to write their reports whilst I concentrate on taking my meds.

So before I bore you all to tears I will put a few short descriptons of the types/areas

Ileocolic:Ileocolitis is the most common type of Crohn's disease. It affects the small intestine, which is known as the ileum, and the colon. The symptoms for someone who has ileocolitis would generally be considerable weight loss, diarrhoea, and cramping or pain in the middle or lower right part of the abdomen.

Terminal ileal: This type of Crohn's disease would affect the last part of the small bowel which is called the ileum. Symptoms of this are the same as ileocolitis as well as fistulas. Also inflammatory abscesses, may form in the lower right section of the abdomen.

Upper gastrointestinal: This covers two types of Crohns disease, duodenum (the beginning of the small intestine) and jejunum (the longest part of the small intestine), these are in the first parts of the small intestine. People with these types of Crohn's disease tend to suffer with nausea, weight loss, and loss of appetite. Also, if the narrow areas of bowel are obstructed, they experience vomiting. With the Jejunum sufferers will often present with malnutrition symptoms as this is where most of the goodness from food is absorbed.

   Colonic: This type of Crohn's disease involves only the colon. Generally the symptoms include skin lesions, joint pains, diarrhoea, rectal bleeding, and the formation of ulcers, fistulas, and abscesses around the anus.

I've tried my best to give a short overview of each of these types of Crohns disease and I'm sure each type will have their own complications. I'm sure we all know none of us have the same story despite having the same illness.

There are many other parts of the digestive tract and many other symptoms that can occur with Crohns however I wanted to give a brief overview of the main areas/types.

So as promised this blog is about the

#GetYourBellyOut campaign behind the scenes, who came up with what and what we get upto so here goes

I will start with who is who... There is Sahara who posted a picture on twitter of her belly after she saw the #nomakeupselfie for cancer and wanted to try and raise awareness of IBD. Sahara then found Gemma on a Facebook site who was already raising money for CCUK and had become a tad disheartened. Someone had been super mean to her on another forum. TUT TUT Victoria is a blogger who came across the first 2 when she was on twitter. Victoria came up with the now infurmus hashtag #GetYourBellyOut, then there is me.. I'm all for building a support network and a place where fellow IBDers can go to get support advice and have abit of a laugh. I had the idea of a facebook page which is doing very well and people seem to be getting a lot out of it. Vic and Sahara both have blogs which go into their roles within the campaign which im sure you have already read so I wont delve into them but below I've added their links so you can have a read.

Victoria's blog is   colitisandme.blogspot.com

Sahara's blog is   http://sahara88uk.blog.com

We all speak to each other only via one very long message on Facebook. We have NEVER met each other or spoken to each other over the phone. I find it incredible how much 4 girls that have met on social media have achieved, we are all very grateful for everyones support and words of encouragement. I for one find it very rewarding knowing I'm helping people and that they now have a good support network that they feel they can turn to.

https://www.facebook.com/getyourbellyout

So what's it like on this super long inbox message… Well a bit like having a good old gossip with friends whilst running a global campaign. It can be hard work at times and hilarious at other times .

Although it can be hard work as we have lots going on in the pipeline I speak for us all when I say we love it and have grown very close to each other plus we all have the same focus…RAISE MORE AWARENESS OF IBD

We all have equal imput and ideas some fab some good some not so good and we all work out which to run with. We are very much of the mind set get things done and I think because we all have IBD we make allowances and support each other, if one of us feels like crap the others take up the slack… None of us are well I swear we wouldn't make a healthy body if you put us all together haha.

We have become close friends, and I think this helps the campaign massively we are all very approachable and want to help as many people as possible… oh and we all think we are comedians.. obviously I'm the funniest!!

The conversations that go on when we get chance (usually a Friday night when we are all exhausted and go a tad crazy) are hilarious! There was one conversation last week in which a member of the team was asked out on a date.. it was kindly turned down to which a response was sent asking the following or words similar…(I'm laughing just writing this) can you actually have a boyfriend? do you have sex like a normal person? I mean if you can't don't worry I can deal with a no sex relationship….(I'm laughing so hard right now my stitches are hurting) to which she wrote.. yes of course I can have a boyfriend and yes I can have sex I've lost my bowel not my vagina!!!

Gemma and Victoria are welsh and decided to teach myself and Sahara a bit of the lingo…I commented that when I go to Snowden they speak welsh in the shop and I'd love to know how to say thank you, as I was writing this unknown to me Sahara had asked what the welsh word for bum and penis were.. (bum is pen ol and penis is Pidyn) anyway I'd not noticed and I said ok so when I buy a cheese and ham baguette I say cheese and ham baguette pen ol pidyn.. well it erupted into fits of laughter I had no idea why until I was told what it meant. I swear none of us could get our breaths it was hilarious I was crying I was laughing that much… imagine I walked into a shop and said that I would have been strung up.

We have quite a few jokes with Sahara too we call her the boss cause that's what seems to be perceived by the media. The truth is there is no boss we all do what is needed when its needed we all have equal say and input. I thinks that's why we all work together well.

My nickname is Princess.. I've no idea why.. probably cause I'm always shopping. Victoria's is pebbles as she spent forever telling us that she felt like she had a pebble in her throat. Gemma's is Gemmy Gem Gem cause she is a dimond a very nice girl that's come massively out of her shell since starting this campaign.

We have so much gratitude for the #GetYourBellyOut groupies and are overwhelmed by the support and thank you comments we have received. We have all balled our eyes out on one or more occasion throughout the campaign from the first takeover to the video below

The Video has also had almost 2000 views to date which is a fantastic success and growing by the day.

Right well I best bugger off now got a campaign to run.. lots in the pipeline to organise.

Thank you for reading and I hope its given you a little more insite of what goes on behind the scenes and how it works… we are just about as crazy as crazy gets but it works!

Stay well love and hugs Lorna xxx

The Belly Crew

A poem by
Rich Williamson

Four ladies, one campaign,

The Belly Crew that keep us sane.

Raised so far £11k,

And getting higher every day.

Lots of bellies, lots of friends,

We're winning but no-one pretends

How far we have still to go;

To raise awareness, Lordy no!

Facebook, Twitter, everywhere!

We'll have it covered, stop and stare;

Marvel at our lovely bellies,

Toiletselfies, on your tellies.

No-one makes us prouder,

So let's all make it louder:

Everyone shout,

#GetYourBellyOut!

Special Thanks to;

All who involved themselves in creating this book, and those who contributed in any way to life experiences voiced in this material.

<u>Matthew Williamson would like to additionally thank;</u>

Amy Southwell for always being my rock through it all.

Hannah Walker for the phenomenal artwork

And my family and friends for just helping through the tough times, no matter what.

Printed in Great Britain
by Amazon.co.uk, Ltd.,
Marston Gate.